Cake on the Floor

Ramsey Bergeron

DEDICATION

In memory of Baxter

CONTENTS

ACKNOWLEDGMENTS

To Daron and Marcus, friendships which have spanned decades, and possibly lifetimes. To Owen, for giving me my first break. Aaron, for our workouts that turn into discourses on philosophy. Paul and Teri for always being willing guinea pigs for workshops and classes. To Ed, who has shown me that age bears no meaning regarding friendships. To Mark and Pat, for being my second set of parents in Arizona. To Ash for our continued civility, even though I broke my promise to never give her up, never let her down, never run around or desert her. To Andi, who has the least amount of free time of any human I know but spent a chunk of it helping me edit and fine-tune this book. My brother, Daniel, who has shown me incredible grace and maturity. And to my mom, who raised two boys in the most challenging of circumstances.

I am eternally grateful to Eddy, whose friendship in life and loss in death have helped me learn the value of being present.

Thank you to the Heroes of Ashcroft and all the generations who came before for allowing me the freedom to explore my creativity. Shaping our shared fictional world allowed me to develop the skills to paint a picture in the real one.

Thank you to the Universe for clearing my path of the things that do not serve me and for lots and lots of cake.

Preface

This is a book about cake on the floor. More specifically, it's about what I learned watching a bride respond to her wedding cake crashing to the floor during her wedding reception. I share this because I feel it's important to set your expectations about the content of this book. Expectations are a funny thing. When I was DJing that wedding over a decade ago, none of us expected that 4-tier cake to come crashing down to the dancefloor. The cake didn't care. It fell anyway.

Now that you're *aware* of what the book's about, I want to emphasize one of the book's central themes, which is, quite frankly... awareness itself. How would *you* have reacted if it was *your* wedding cake on *your* wedding day? It's easy to think you wouldn't care. After all, you have no emotional connection to a story you about a newlywed couple you never met. Pause for a moment and *really* think about it. Go ahead... I'll wait.

pause

What factors did you consider when determining how you would respond? What emotions were at play? What was the significance of the cake? Why did I ask you how you would have 'reacted' in the last paragraph but asked how you would have 'responded' in this one? What's the difference? Everything. No exaggeration, the difference between reacting and responding will determine if your legacy is written by default or by design.

Looking back at your life so far, how have you handled the unexpected? How much conscious choice went into it? I suppose it depends if you are one of the 95% of people who think they are self-aware or one of the 10-15% who actually are.*

If, up to now, you have not been as aware as you would like, try not to *judge* yourself. This book is also about judgment, which I will cover in Chapter 2. When we assign value and *think* things "should" or "shouldn't" have happened, it prevents us from accepting reality. I'll cover how we think in Chapter 5.

---

*Based on the research of Dr. Tasha Eurich, an organizational psychologist and author of Insight: The Surprising Truth About How Others See Us, How We See Ourselves, and Why the Answers Matter More Than We Think (2020)

Take the Medicine

There may be concepts in this book that you hear for the first time. You've managed to survive in life this long knowing what you know, and when you receive new information that may challenge some of your current beliefs or ways of thinking, it may cause you discomfort (I'll dive more into why that is in a later chapter). To help you keep an open mind, I want to share a story I learned during a meditation retreat regarding our personal knowledge.

There are three types of knowledge: Knowledge you are told, knowledge you intellectualize, and knowledge you experience. Let's view these through the lens of going to a doctor when you are sick.

You go to the doctor, tell her what's wrong, and she writes you a prescription that she says will make you better. So, you go home, put the prescription on an altar, pour rose petals around it, pray to it, and pray to the doctor, thanking her for giving you the means to get better. The only catch is, you don't get better. That's an example of knowledge you are told.

Since you're still sick, you return to the doctor and ask how the medicine will make you better. She explains how the medicine is designed to combat your ailment and the pathway in which it operates. So you go home, show the prescription to your neighbors, and tell them how great your doctor is! You tell them how the medicine works and how, when you take this medicine, you will get better! You have taken the knowledge, and you have an intellectual understanding of it.

But the only way to have an experiential understanding of the medicine and how it can help you is to take the medicine.

In this book, I have done the best I can to share my experiencial understanding of how to handle life's unexpected moments with resilience and grace. Reading it gives you an understanding of how medicine works. It's up to you to decide if you take it.

In hindsight, this book is about so much more than a cake on the floor. It's about your legacy. By reading this book, you will be able to view even the most challenging situations with curiosity and ease, allowing you to live intentionally. As you read on, I encourage you to reflect on your own experiences with expectations and disappointments. Recall moments when your expectations collided with reality, and consider how you responded. I'll share the same powerful tools I've shared with my clients for over a decade to help you create space - that magical pause - in which you get to determine who you want to be. You will learn to separate yourself from your thoughts and emotions and view them objectively, giving you true emotional intelligence and freedom from intrusive thoughts. I will demystify the most overused word of the 21st century: mindfulness. To help you shape your story, I will share parts of my experience as a coach, an athlete, a speaker, and most importantly, a human who has been humbled by experiencing profound loss.

Charles R Swindoll said, "Life is 10% what happens to us and 90% how we react to it." I forgive Charles for not acknowledging our option to respond. But you get the idea.

Life is full of the unexpected. Of uncertainty. Of change.

There is always cake on the floor.

Ramsey Bergeron
1/26/24

CHAPTER 1

THE UNEXPECTED

"BLESSED IS HE WHO EXPECTS NOTHING, FOR HE SHALL NEVER BE DISAPPOINTED."

— ALEXANDER POPE

This was not what we expected. A newlywed bride, knife in hand, standing over the ruins of her extravagant wedding cake, splattered across the reception hall floor.

Few events are as meticulously planned as a wedding. Every detail, from the colors of the napkins to the centerpieces to the music, is carefully curated by the happy couple (aka the bride). Moonlighting as a DJ and planner for over 20 years, I helped set and manage expectations for over 800 weddings and receptions. I've seen a bride make her grand entrance via helicopter, a donkey for a ring bearer, and everything in between. The planning and coordination between venue, DJ, caterer, and photographer (and, in the examples above, pilots and animal handlers) culminate in what everyone hopes will be a flawless evening.

So, when this particular bride went to cut the cake on that fateful day, and the legs of the table buckled, everyone in the room froze. Over three hundred guests, wide-eyed, silently stared at her. We waited on bated breath for her to scream and curse the heavens for ruining her wedding day. After all, *that's* what we were expecting. But that scream never came. Looking at the collapsed cake, she took a deep breath and, after a moment, burst out laughing. Everyone else followed suit, and soon, the room was filled with the laughter of hundreds of carefree guests. The cake falling on the floor became the highlight.

Expectations

One of the things that gives us the most peace in our lives is having an expectation of what comes next. It gives us a sense of control and stability. It allows us to plan, set, and achieve meaningful goals in our personal and professional lives. When our expectations are met and align with reality, we feel good! You want to get a promotion, so you work hard, take on extra projects, and, lo and behold, get promoted. But what happens when you don't get that promotion? When the proverbial cake in your life ends up on the floor? That can be a much harder pill to swallow. But it doesn't have to be.

Thumbing a Ride

In 2018, I loaded up my bike and headed across the Atlantic to compete in Ironman Norway. It was my 9th full-distance triathlon, and I was ready. I felt fantastic except for a thumb injury I got a few months prior from a ski accident, but it wasn't anything I was expecting to affect my ability to swim, bike, or run.

Race morning came around, and everything was off to a perfect start. I finished the 2.4-mile swim in near record time and set out on my bike to conquer the 112-mile course before tackling the ensuing marathon. I expected the bike to be challenging as it was through the rolling hills of Norway's fjord lands, but the scenery and my visualizations of success helped me push through. I had trained for months listening to Bill Withers' "Lovely Day" and repeatedly sang that song with every pedal stroke. It has a good rhythm to keep my cycling tempo consistent, and it was, in fact, a lovely day. Glancing at my watch, I was headed for what could have been a PR (personal record).

Then everything fell apart.

At mile 36, I got a flat. My injured thumb, which I wasn't expecting to be an issue, became quite the burden, and changing the tire without its use was not easy. It was so 'not easy' that I didn't do it right at all. There was a slight bulge on one side of the tire that I didn't notice till it was fully inflated. (If you know nothing about riding a bike, having a bulge on your tire is NOT good. Your perfectly round circle now has a lump preventing it from rolling smoothly.)

As I started to ride again, the obvious bulge in the tire "thwapped" with every tire rotation. I could hear and feel it, and when I increased speed, it did as well. A constant reminder of my screw-up. It took me 15 minutes to change the tire, and I was flustered. This was not at all what I was expecting.

Without options, I pressed on. I could still get off the bike in a respectable time and knock on wood; my patch job was holding up, at least for the time being. I made it about 15 more miles before the tire exploded on a downhill section at about 32 MPH. By the grace of God, I didn't wreck, and slowly applied my brakes and pulled to the side of the course. I knew it would be bad, but I had no idea how bad. The whole sidewall of the outer tire had blown out. (For those of you who don't ride bikes, it's akin to driving a car without the rubber tire on the wheel). I was on a section of the course that wasn't on a main road but more of a bike path down by one of the lakes. I waited and waited for a SAG wagon (a roving vehicle on courses that provides mechanical assistance to racers) to come by.

One never did.

Out of CO2 and tubes, and with a shredded tire, I only had a few options. Fellow racers slowed and offered what help they could provide, but when I tried to fill another tube in the tire, it exploded immediately.

I knew my race was over. Bill Withers and his Lovely Day could go to hell. Fate had conspired to crush my expectations of a picture-perfect race. I was angry... furious even. I was ready for this race! I had trained for months and spent thousands of dollars! My FRIENDS spent a lot of money to *watch* me do this. This was not how it was supposed to go!!!!

Sitting on the side of a Norwegian bike path for three hours with no phone and nothing to do but look out at the countryside, I had a lot of time to think. Finally, a thought occurred to me. I held up my two hands as fists about shoulder width apart and looked at them. If one hand is my "expectations," the things I want to have happen or should have happened, and the other hand is reality; the gap between them is stress. That's all mental stress really is—the gap between expectations and reality.

My tire exploding wasn't what was making me upset. What upset me was my expectation that my tire was not *supposed to* explode. My expectation was that *there would be* a SAG wagon to provide support. My expectation was that *I was going to finish* the race. It wasn't supposed to be this way! Yet... this was the way it was.

I was so focused on what was "supposed" to happen I wasn't aware of where I was. I took a moment and looked around. The sun was shining, it was around 70 degrees, and I was sitting in a valley with towering walls of fjords around me. It was magnificent.

The Lesson or the Loss

At first glance, it may seem like having unmet expectations is a no-win proposition, so why set myself up to feel bad by setting a goal I may not hit?

Having something to aim for and look forward to is a massive part of what gives our life meaning and purpose. We get married and order a giant cake to cut because we have faith that the marriage will last and that we can enjoy the cake as a part of the celebration. I signed up for Ironman Norway because I expected to cross the finish line and put another medal on my wall.

But regardless of whether or not the marriage lasts, the cake collapses, or the finish line is crossed, there are still valuable lessons to be learned along the way. Life is so much more than the boxes we check. It's the journey we undertake to check those boxes. It's how we learn, grow, and experience the situations we encounter. It's called "the hero's journey" and not "the hero's destination" for a reason.

It boils down to what you choose to focus on. Are you focusing on the lesson or the loss? Even though I didn't finish the Ironman that day, having the expectation of finishing allowed me to get in shape, allowed me to experience the wonderful country of Norway, and provided me with joy and meaning for months leading up to it. Even though my marriage ended in divorce, I spent nearly a decade with an incredible woman and experienced a lot of joy and growth along the way. The hardships and disagreements in that marriage taught me so much about myself. Habits I needed to unlearn, what I really wanted in a partner, and what kind of partner I wanted to be. If I were so focused on the fact the marriage didn't last, I would not be able to see what the experience taught me.

It's easier to see the positive in situations when time has passed and you have the opportunity to reflect on the wisdom you have (hopefully) gained. But what about in the heat of the moment? When you are standing there staring at the cake that has just fallen to the floor? It depends on your perspective.

Maybe Yes, Maybe No

There is an old Chinese proverb about a farmer who lost his prize horse. When his neighbor heard about the horse running away, he came to the farmer and said," Oh no! That's terrible for you!"

"Maybe yes, maybe no," the farmer replied.

A few days later, the horse returned to the farm with another horse following him. "That's fantastic!" exclaimed the neighbor.

"Maybe yes, maybe no," said the farmer.

The next day, the farmer's son fell and broke his leg while trying to tame the new horse. "Oh no!" said the neighbor. "That's terrible!"

"Maybe yes, maybe no," said the farmer.

Shortly after, the army came through their small village, looking to recruit all able-bodied men to go to war. With his leg in a cast, the farmer's son was spared having to fight. "That's terrific," exclaimed the neighbor yet again.

"Maybe yes, maybe no."

This story perfectly encapsulates how seemingly "negative" things can sometimes create "positive" results. We never know how something will turn out, so why do we have such an adverse reaction when things do not go as planned?

There is Always Cake on The Floor

No matter how well you structure your life, there will always be cake on the floor. Cake on the floor is getting sick the day you are supposed to go on vacation. Cake on the floor is a cancer diagnosis. It's your pet passing away. It's losing money on an investment. It's getting passed over for a promotion. It's a tire that explodes in the middle of a race. Sometimes, it's literal cake on a literal floor. Anything that happens in your life that you didn't expect to happen is cake on the floor. There will always be cake on the floor because of the one constant that will always be there: Change.

Change

If you're reading this book, it's fairly safe to say that you have at least an intellectual and somewhat experiential understanding of change. After all, change happens every single moment of every single day. It's the only constant. But to have a truly experiential understanding of it and how it affects you, you have to gain an awareness of all the ways change manifests.

Not only is change constant, but every single thing in existence is in a constant state of change. Even what you consider permanent, like a mountain or the really bad tattoo on your arm, will change shape, form, and appearance depending on the time scale. It's all a matter of perspective. As such, I will use the words "impermanent" and "change" interchangeably. Let's think about impermanence and how our expectations cause us disappointment in one of 3 main ways:

#1 Expecting Things Not to Change

The older most of us get, the more we like things the way they are. It's comfortable and familiar and doesn't require much mental energy to grasp. But when something we think of as a 'constant' changes, it can cause us to react poorly. Ironically, it's not the change itself that's the source of the problem. It's our false belief that things stay the same.

Thich Nhat Hahn, one of the world's greatest modern-day masters of mindfulness, said it best: "It is not impermanence that makes us suffer, what makes us suffer is wanting things to be permanent when they are not."

Let's say they roll out new software at your office (or, God forbid, Facebook updates their interface. The nerve!). As much as we all say we want new technology, we tend to complain when it happens.

Like it or not, right now, sitting here reading this book, you are the youngest you will ever be. Some people have a hard time with this notion. We lament that we are aging as if there were some alternative. We suffer when we don't accept the natural aging process, whether it's ourselves or those we love.

Shortly after I moved to Arizona, I rescued an incredible Jack Russell mix named Charlie. Charlie was one of the most active dogs I had ever seen, climbing mountains with me and even able to run up trees. Soon after he turned ten, his health began to decline rather quickly. My girlfriend at the time and I both loved him very much and were sad to see our once able-bodied buddy lose his hearing and struggle to walk. At times, I would see her holding him, crying, and sad about his imminent decline. As hard as it was, I encouraged her to be here with him. Yes, his health was declining, but he is here *now*. Let's celebrate his life. Either way, he is going to pass one day, so we can either make the most of where he is or spend the last few years of his life with him, watching us cry every day.

Whether it's losing pets or parents or watching our children get older, we all want to hold onto precious moments. We fail to realize that these moments don't last forever, *which is exactly what makes them so precious!* If you spend your time in the middle of the precious moment wishing it lasted longer, you aren't even enjoying the moment itself! Expecting things to stay the same doesn't keep change from happening; it only delays our ability to accept reality and find peace when it does.

#2: Expecting Things to Change Immediately.

Oh, the noble American pursuit of immediate gratification. Spending almost two decades in the physical wellness industry, I saw this play out almost daily. As much as I would try to manage their expectations, clients couldn't understand why they didn't lose weight after eating salads for lunch for a week!

"How long does it take to grow a human baby?" I would ask them.

"Around nine months," they usually reply with a puzzled look.

"With all the advances in medical science, if the mom tried really hard, could she get it down to 3 or 4 months?" I asked dryly. They saw where I was going with it.

Things take as long as they take. Just because we expect something to be fast doesn't make it so. I deal with this a lot, working with managers in my capacity as an executive coach. They are frustrated their employees aren't learning or improving their skills at the rate the manager wants them to. If the manager has children, I ask them to tell me about when their children were learning to walk. Did they yell at them or ask them what was wrong when they stumbled?

"You should have this by now!" I jokingly say, pretending to be a parent yelling at a stumbling toddler. Usually, they laugh and say no, it's just a part of the process. The same thing applies to adults. How long does it take someone to learn a new skill? As long as it takes. Just because you learned it in two months doesn't mean everyone else will.

#3: Things Change, but Not How You Wanted

In this example, we can accept that things will change, but our expectation of how the change will occur is unmet. Returning to the story of the cake on the floor, what would have been the best-case scenario had the cake not fallen? In less than an hour, the wedding guests would have devoured it! Either way, the cake was going to be gone. We are upset that the cake wasn't impermanent in the way that we wanted it to be. What if no one ate the cake, and it sat there for another three weeks? We would be upset if it were still there!

Let's say you head to work, and they announce in a morning meeting that they are finally moving forward with the reorg you have been anticipating for months. You are okay with the fact that change is taking place, but when you learn that some of the responsibilities you enjoyed are going away, you get upset. It's your version of the farmer losing his horse. Will the reorg be a good thing? Maybe yes, maybe no.

"Hurry"

The greatest example of change that we struggle to accept is also one of the most natural: death.

In June 2020, shortly after the COVID pandemic shut down the world, I got word that my best friend was on a ventilator in the hospital. He didn't have the COVID-19 virus, but due to isolation and having battled depression and excessive drinking for most of his adult life, he drank himself into a coma. I wasn't able to get updates directly from the hospital staff, but his mother would call and fill me in on how he was doing. Some days, it sounded like he was improving; others, it did not.

When I saw her number on my caller ID on July 1st of that year, I thought it would be another standard update. Instead, it was a call I will never forget. She had finally made the decision to take him off the ventilator. She gave me the cell phone number of his nurse and told me to call and say my goodbyes.

Dealing with situations like this during the early days of the pandemic was such a surreal experience. Hospitals weren't taking outside calls, so the only way to be able to speak to anyone admitted was to call the cell phones of their caretakers. I called the nurse, who answered immediately. Eddy's mom was kind enough to tell her to expect my call. She put me on speakerphone. I could hear Eddy's ragged, exasperated breathing as his body was shutting down without the help of the ventilator.

I bawled to him. The truth is, I don't remember a single thing I was saying at the time. All I can remember is the uncontrollable sobbing. After several minutes, the nurse took me off speakerphone and said she had to attend to other patients. I begged and pleaded with her to please let me see him. I knew hospitals weren't letting people in to say goodbye to their loved ones, but I had to try. She said she doubted she could but would call me back if it was possible. I hung up, resigned that I would never see my friend again.

Within a minute, my phone buzzed to life. I recognized the nurse's number.

"Hurry."

It was all she had to say. I covered myself in PPE and found myself in his hospital room 20 minutes later. I was the only visitor he had for his entire month-long stay on or off the ventilator. The only person who was allowed to visit him during that time was his mother, and as a cancer survivor, she opted not to due to her severely compromised immune system.

I sat at his bedside and held his hand. I told him how sorry I was that I couldn't help him. I apologized for the times I wasn't a good friend. When I was selfish or mean. I thanked him for all the times he was there for me when I needed a friend. I reminisced about the great times we had together, starting from when we met playing soccer when we were five years old in rural Arkansas. I made jokes that I knew he would love and others I knew he would roll his eyes at if he could. I asked the nurse to put the TV on a news station I knew Eddy hated, hoping to see him sit up and yell at the TV because he was faking.

He was not.

He didn't say a word, but I knew with every fiber of my being that he could hear me. That wherever his mind was, my voice was guiding him. After being at his side for five hours, I knew it was time to say goodbye. I told him that I understood if he needed to go. I didn't want him to be in pain. I loved him, I would always love him, and I would never forget him. As I continued to cry and hold his hand, he took his final breath and passed away.

Even though I consider myself extremely fortunate to say goodbye to my friend the way I did, I wish he didn't suffer. But because his death was drawn out, I got to say everything I wanted and be there with him as he transitioned. Other deaths in my life were very different.

I love my animal companions as much as (let's be honest, sometimes more than) most people. Three years after Eddy passed, I found Baxter, my beloved Min-pin sidekick, after he had already crossed the rainbow bridge. That morning, he was happy, wagging his tail and greeting me with his trademark lip bite with no indication it was his last day. In shock and disbelief, I picked him up from where he had collapsed next to his bed and rushed to the vet in a vain attempt to resuscitate him. It was too late. The vet said that he most likely had a heart attack and died quickly and peacefully. Even though I was thankful that he didn't have to suffer and that I didn't have to decide that it was his time to go, I felt robbed that I didn't get to say goodbye.

Death is the greatest change of all. And even though we know it is coming, we have difficulty accepting it or how it happened. We always think it would be better if they passed differently. We want to be able to say goodbye and apologize, but we don't want them to suffer. On the other hand, we want them to have a quick, peaceful death, but if we didn't know it was coming, we wouldn't have the opportunity to say goodbye. All around, it is an incredibly complex situation for us to process and accept.

Whether it's something as trivial as a cake falling to the floor or something as life-altering as the death of a loved one, it is important to learn how to separate the facts from our judgment of the facts to help us gain clarity and accept the reality of unexpected situations.

CHAPTER 1 REFLECTION QUESTIONS

Reflection on Unmet Expectations:
Think about a time when something important didn't go as planned in your life. How did you react initially, and how do you view that event now? What did you learn from the experience?

The Gap Between Expectations and Reality:
Reflect on a recent situation where your expectations did not align with reality. What was the 'gap' between your expectations and what actually happened? How did this gap affect your emotions and actions?

Adapting to Change:
Consider a significant change you've experienced recently. How did you adapt to this change? What strategies did you use to cope, and what might you do differently next time?

Perspective on 'Cake on the Floor' Moments:
Can you think of a 'cake on the floor' moment in your life? How did you respond? In hindsight, what positive outcomes or lessons emerged from that experience?

Goals and Expectations:
Reflect on a goal you set that you did not achieve. What

expectations did you have for yourself, and how did you handle the outcome? How has this shaped your approach to setting goals since?

Impermanence and Change:
How do you typically react to change, especially when it's unexpected? What does this say about your view on impermanence, and how might you cultivate a more adaptable attitude toward change?

Joy and Meaning in the Journey:
Looking back on an ambitious project or goal you undertook, regardless of the outcome, what joy and meaning did you find in the journey? How does this perspective influence your current ambitions?

Fear of Failing:
How has a fear of failing prevented you from pursuing something because you might fail at it?

Learning from Loss:
Think of a loss you've experienced. What did this loss teach you about yourself, your values, and how you relate to others? How has this lesson influenced your actions moving forward?

The Hero's Journey:

In what ways do you see your life as a 'hero's journey'? What challenges have you faced, and how have they transformed you? What does 'the hero's destination' look like for you now?

CHAPTER 2

FACT VS. JUDGMENT

"GET YOUR FACTS FIRST, THEN YOU CAN DISTORT THEM AS
YOU PLEASE."

— MARK TWAIN

In June 2023, I returned to endurance sports by swimming 12.5 miles around Key West, Florida. This was my first epic race since I started embracing the cake on the floor and, by far, the most challenging physical event I had ever attempted. For starters, you weren't allowed to wear a wetsuit, which would have provided additional buoyancy. The race was also over 10 miles longer than the longest swim I had ever competed in. (The most brutal endurance events I had done up to that point were Ironman triathlons, and the swim portion of those races was "only" 2.4 miles.)

I had completed numerous ocean swims before, including a yearly Olympic triathlon in Malibu, so sharks had never been something that I was overly concerned with. While competing in Ironman Cairns, the swim took place over the Great Barrier Reef, and sharks were the number FOUR thing to worry about (in order: jellyfish, crocodiles, stingrays, *then* sharks). Though the Key West swim was the longest I would be in the water, I wouldn't have to go it alone. Marcus, a good friend I've known since college, was set to kayak alongside me the whole way to provide me with nutrition and navigation. The course description on the website also put my mind at ease, as the water was crystal clear and shallow, ranging from 4 to 12 ft.

As the starting whistle went off and I navigated through the breakers, I was confident I would finish the race. I was well rested, I could see the bottom, and Marcus was by my side. I found a rhythm for several hours, remaining in each moment and taking it one stroke at a time. I was in an almost zen-like state, casually observing the seaweed swaying in the tide as I could hear the air from each breath bubble past my ears.

Unexpectedly (those pesky 'expectations' again), around eight miles in, the sea floor… disappeared. A channel had been cut between Key West and the adjacent Stock Island to allow larger boat traffic. The water temperature went from upper 80 degrees to bone-chilling in an instant. The swaying seaweed had been replaced with the nothingness of the deep.

My heart began racing uncontrollably. The thought of "I am about to be eaten by a shark" consumed me (pun not intended, but hilarious). My instinct (how I wanted to react) was to get out of the water immediately. My monkey mind (more on that later) told me to climb up on the kayak for safety, but that was not an option. It was only a one-person kayak occupied by Marcus and had two additional coolers strapped to it filled with our food and water.

At that moment, I wished I was one of those lizards that could run across the water's surface, making it to the far shore in seconds instead of the several hours I had left. If I did not calm myself down soon, I would have a full-blown panic attack, causing me to flail in the water (which anyone who watches Shark Week knows will attract more maneaters). Even though it has been extinct for millennia, my thoughts told me a megalodon, the largest shark that ever lived, was going to swallow Marcus and me whole.

Thankfully, I was able to pause. I slowed my breathing and talked to myself. I reminded myself that I had seen sharks while swimming numerous times before. The month prior, while training for this race in Kona, Hawaii, smaller reef sharks minded their own business a dozen feet below me. Statistically speaking, shark attacks are incredibly rare.

At the end of the day, what is within my control? All I could do at that very moment was swim. One stroke at a time. So, I did. Sure enough, after an eternity (20 minutes to the casual observer), the other side of the channel emerged from the depths, and I was back in shallow water.

Certainty that I will be eaten by a shark:

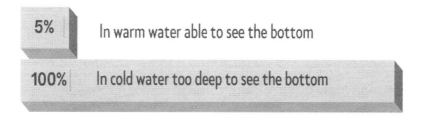

Often, we suffer much more in our imagination than in reality. It wasn't a shark that caused me to panic and nearly quit the race. It was the *fear* of a shark, based on no evidence of a shark (man-eating, extinct, or otherwise) even being present.

Separating Fact from Judgment

Most of what we "think" is a combination of facts and judgments. On the surface, they may appear the same. However, it's important to understand the substantial yet sometimes nuanced differences between the two.

Facts are the objective raw data of the world around us. Think of them as clinical observations based on evidence that is repeatable, verifiable, and devoid of emotion. They possess an inherent neutrality. Facts, by themselves, do not create strong emotions. Sharks live in the ocean: fact. I am swimming in the ocean: fact. The water became colder and deeper: fact.

On the other hand, judgments are personal and subjective *interpretations or opinions* influenced by emotions, thoughts, and previous experiences. They may be based on facts, or they may be complete speculation, not based on reality. If you notice you are having a strong emotional reaction to something, it probably is a judgment of a fact. This cold, deep water is terrifying, I know a shark is going to eat me: judgment. I don't belong out here, I have to get out of the water right now: judgment. There might be a megalodon that survived extinction down there: judgment.

Judgment vs Discernment

Judgments can also be assigning a value to something that innately lacks value. Words like *good, bad, better than*, or *worse than* are all phrases that indicate judgment.

Discernment, however, is simply indicating something is different, based on fact, without assigning a value. It is discernment to say my car is not a bicycle. It is a judgment to say my car is *better than* a bicycle. That's personal and subjective, as well as assigning value. Better how? Maybe it's faster but also more expensive, requires gasoline, and releases pollutants. The farmer's horse is no longer at the farm: discernment. It's bad that the farmer's horse ran away: judgment. When we start using phrases like *good, bad, better than*, or *worse than*, we move away from objective fact and towards personal judgment.

My knowledge of sharks and their existence in the ocean were facts. I'm not assigning a value saying it is "good" or "bad" that there are sharks in the ocean (which would be judgments.) Factually, I can only state that they are there. However, my worry about encountering sharks, fueled by fear and anxiety, was a judgment—an interpretation of those facts.

I can discern that my cake is on the floor. "My wedding is ruined" (the emotional nature of this statement should be a hint) is a judgment. Similarly, we frequently intermingle facts and judgments in our daily lives, and it's essential to discern between them.

How Judgment Distorts Reality

A client of mine, Amy, was convinced she was getting fired. One Friday morning, she noticed her boss whispering to a few of her colleagues and could tell the conversation had changed quickly and awkwardly whenever she entered the room. Her fears became more elevated when she found out she had been left off several emails that day regarding projects she had traditionally been involved with. She felt blindsided, hurt, and confused. She had always received praise for her contributions and was convinced this was being done because she was a woman. Everyone else still involved in the project was a man. She grew more and more angry as the day went on. When her boss asked her to come to his office near the end of the day, her anxiety went into overdrive.

Fearing the inevitable, she decided she wasn't going without a fight. She marched into his office where he sat, leaning back in his chair, smiling, with his arms crossed. "How dare you," she blurted out before he could even say a word. "After everything I have done for this company, you are firing me?"

"Not at all," he replied. "We are promoting you." She then noticed the bottle of her favorite wine sitting on his desk with a bow. She was mortified.

Her boss went on to tell her she was left off the emails because the projects would not be a part of her new responsibilities as a supervisor. The perceived whispering was the boss asking some of her coworkers what her favorite type of wine was so he could gift it to her when he surprised her with the promotion news. Needless to say, her judgment of the facts was what we worked on during her next session.

She was left off of emails she would have been included in in the past: fact. That must mean she is getting fired: judgment. Being unable to separate the facts from the judgment caused her so much stress that it nearly created a self-fulfilling prophecy!

I have another client who says he hates his job. Because he views hating his job as a fact, he goes to work every day believing he hates it there. Therefore, his attitude, work ethic, and actions become that of someone who, indeed, does hate his job. But when I ask him to describe what he hates about his job, I find out that what he really hates is his hour-and-a-half commute. The job itself is fine, but he is so worked up by the time he arrives and dreads the return commute so deeply during the whole day that he spends all day feeling he hates his job. It becomes a self-fulfilling prophecy. He has made his judgment his reality.

Armed with this new awareness that he dislikes his commute, he decides to ask his boss if he can work remotely for three days a week and gets approval. Now, he finds he is much more content, productive, and a pleasure to be around at work and at home. It's the same job, and he's doing the same work. It turns out it wasn't the job he hated. However, he was unable to respond in a meaningful way until he was able to separate the facts from the judgments of the situation.

Non-Judgment

"When you go out into the woods, and you look at trees, you see all these different trees. And some of them are bent, and some of them are straight, and some of them are evergreens, and some of them are whatever. And you look at the tree and you allow it. You see why it is the way it is."
- Ram Dass

In Eastern philosophy, viewing things without judgment is known as practicing "non-judgment." It is the practice of viewing things as they are and not assigning "good" or "bad" labels to them. This can be an arduous task.

Whenever I begin to tell the cake on the floor during my speeches, the audience tenses up the second I mention that the leg of the cake table was not locked out. They already feel a cake falling on the floor is "bad." But the reality is that it's not good or bad; it just... is. We will talk about the emotional component of judgment in Chapter 5.

CHAPTER 2 REFLECTION QUESTIONS

Identifying Facts and Judgments:

Think of a recent situation where you felt a strong emotional reaction. Can you separate the facts from the judgments you made about it?

Challenging Personal Judgments:

Recall a time when your judgment about a person or situation turned out to be incorrect. What assumptions did you make, and how did they affect your behavior and feelings at the time?

Understanding the Impact of Judgments:

Consider an aspect of your life you are currently unhappy with. Are your feelings based on facts, or are they influenced by judgments? How might your perception change if you viewed the situation without judgment?

Practicing Discernment:

Reflect on a decision you need to make. How can you apply discernment to distinguish between facts and personal biases to make a more informed choice?

Exploring Non-Judgment:

Spend a few moments observing your surroundings or

thinking about a recent event. Can you describe what you see or recall without applying any labels of "good" or "bad"? How does this change your emotional response to the observation or memory?

Investigating the Source of Judgments:
Identify a judgment you frequently make about yourself or others. What experiences or beliefs might this judgment stem from? How does recognizing this influence your feelings toward that judgment?

Applying Non-Judgment in Daily Life:
What is one way you can practice non-judgment in your daily interactions? How might this practice affect your relationships and communication with others?

Evaluating the Role of Judgments in Stress:
Think about a recent stressful event. To what extent did judgment (your own or others') contribute to the stress? How might the situation have felt different with a non-judgmental approach?

Chapter 3
Reacting vs. Responding

"Our ultimate freedom is the right and power to decide how anybody or anything outside ourselves will affect us."

— **Steven R Covey**

The cake hitting the floor of our life can come in many different shapes and sizes—a sudden change in plans, a frustrating setback at work, or a disagreement with a loved one, and in at least one scenario I experienced, a literal cake falling on the floor. What we do next falls into one of two categories: reacting or responding.

Reacting

Reacting is automatic. It's usually done without conscious thought and tends to be instinctual. Think of this as your "fight or flight" mode. Reacting also tends to be a catabolic process, breaking down body tissue. You may be thinking, "This sounds bad! I don't want to be in fight or flight mode and breaking down body tissue!" Well, maybe sometimes you do. Catabolic energy isn't inherently bad. If you are in an actual life-or-death scenario, like hiking in the woods and a bear starts chasing you, you want catabolic energy. Your body releases cortisol into your system to break down body tissue for fuel to help you outrun the bear.

The times that catabolic energy may not be serving you is when your heart starts racing in situations that are not life-or-death, such as your wedding cake falling on the floor or forgetting to email a report to your boss. Even though you have no chance of dying (short of slipping in the cake and breaking your neck), your mind makes you feel like it is a life-or-death situation. You may even say something like, "My boss is going to kill me!" not even realizing you are just adding fuel to the catabolic fire.

This reemphasizes the importance of being able to separate facts from judgment. Most things we react to are not, in fact, life or death. You may feel like your boss will kill you, but I'm willing to wager that's a judgment.

Reactions don't always rise to the life-or-death level, but they still create a sense that something is wrong and the situation is bad or dangerous.   Let's consider a few more non-cake-related real-life scenarios:

1. **Traffic Jam**: You're driving to an important meeting and suddenly find yourself stuck in a traffic jam. Your immediate reaction might involve frustration, honking your horn, and trying to change lanes hastily.

2. **Miscommunication**: In a conversation with a friend, they make an offhand comment that you interpret as an insult. Your reaction may be to get defensive or storm out.

3. **Sudden Change in Plans**: You've meticulously planned a weekend getaway, only to have it derailed by unexpected bad weather. Your immediate reaction might involve annoyance, irritation, or resentment.

In these scenarios, you can see how reacting may not be in your best interest, but there are also longer-term consequences. Not only does it prevent you from finding solutions, it literally shortens your life! Fight or flight mode is very taxing and unsustainable for long periods of time. There is only so long you can run from the bear (proverbial or otherwise) before you collapse from exhaustion. This is why chronic stress is so deadly. It may start as something mild, like getting sick or feeling run down. Over time, it can lead to disastrous effects like a nervous breakdown or a heart attack.

<u>Responding</u>

Even though it may not feel like it in the moment, responding is a viable alternative to these unexpected situations in life. When you respond, you take a moment to decide how you want to handle the current situation. You take conscious control of your mind, allowing you to behave in ways that align with your values and beliefs. Responding considers the feelings and well-being of yourself and others with a more thoughtful and deliberate approach. It tends to be based on fact. This is how responding may look in the situations above:

1. **Traffic Jam**: You can choose to find another route or be productive with your time by listening to a podcast or calling a friend you've been meaning to catch up.

2. **Miscommunication**: You ask your friend for clarity as to what they meant and realize that what they are sharing is a projection of themself that may not have anything to do with you.

3. **Sudden Change in Plans**: Even though you may not like the change, it's out of your control, so you decide to focus on what you can control instead.

<u>Getting There Eventually</u>

In 2014, I had two Ironman races scheduled six months apart, one in New Zealand and one in Whistler, Canada. About five months before the first of those races, I injured myself while training. I got overzealous, running downhill with a small group of people, and herniated three discs in my back. Having already had two back surgeries, the prospect of a third did not appeal to me. My doctor told me to avoid another surgery I should not run for at least a year.

A year??? What the hell, man? Traveling to New Zealand had been on my bucket list for as long as I could remember (well, at least since the Lord of the Rings movies came out). I had already gotten my plane tickets and hotel for both trips. Thousands of dollars were on the line. My expectations (damn you, expectations!) were crushed.

To say I was upset was an understatement. I spent weeks alternating between anger and shame. I blamed the other runners I was running with the day I injured myself. They were egging me on to run faster, after all! I blamed myself for being so stupid as to stomp down a hill, heel-striking when I knew better. I blamed God for *doing* this to *me*.

Every day after working with my personal training clients (which was now incredibly laborious), I lay in bed, full of hopelessness, and stared at the ceiling. As an athlete, my identity was tied up in what I was able to do. If I wasn't able to race, who was I? I didn't feel like I had any value. I was miserable to be around. I would snap at my poor wife, who was nothing but sympathetic and supportive.

After getting a cortisone shot into my spine, I was able to think a little more clearly. The pain had diminished to the point that I could walk. One day, while walking around the neighborhood, I passed the pool I had been swimming laps in before my injury. A man who had to be in his late seventies was walking up the steps, holding onto the handrail while exiting the pool. Waiting at the top of the steps was his walker with his towel thrown over the top.

A lightbulb went off for me. "Can I swim?" I asked my doctor during a follow-up appointment I had later that week.

He said, "Yes. It's actually good for the back."

"Can I bike?" He nodded his head affirmatively. Sure, as long as you do so in a way that doesn't cause any more compression to the discs." Riding a triathlon bike wasn't an issue. With the way it's designed, I could essentially lay down on top of it, which was a lot more accommodating than a traditional road bike would have been.

So I could swim and bike, and I already knew I was able to walk. I decided I would at least attempt to do both of those Ironman races after all. I would swim and bike, and if I made it to the marathon, I would judge how I felt and walk as much of the 26.2 miles as possible.

With that plan in place, I managed to finish them both, walking every step of both marathons. My time was not as fast as I had wanted it to be, but I was able to enjoy the beautiful scenery and make the most of both experiences. I loved New Zealand so much that I have returned twice since then!

It took weeks for me to separate the facts from the judgment. Weeks spent lashing out in anger I justified because the situation wasn't fair.

Time doesn't heal all wounds. It's what you do with that time that matters. Reacting emotionally and stewing endlessly does nothing to create peace or find solutions to the situation.

Now, without judgment, think of a time in your life when you were eventually able to respond to a situation you initially reacted to. If you're like me, you can probably think of several but try to focus on one.

As you think about it, try not to shame yourself. Again, the name of the game here is awareness. Please don't beat yourself up for not knowing something when you didn't know it. View this as an opportunity to learn about yourself.

As a learning lesson, how much time, energy, money, or other resources did reacting cost you? Maybe it's even still costing you. How would it benefit you to learn how to respond sooner? Maybe even within the moment?

Our Resulting Legacy

The critical distinction between reacting and responding lies in the consequences that follow. When we react without conscious thought, we often make decisions that we later regret. These reactions can escalate conflicts, worsen emotional distress, and lead to impulsive actions that don't serve our best interests.

Have you ever hastily reacted to a situation only to have to explain yourself later? If you've ever said (or even thought), "I don't know why I did that; that is NOT who I am," then you, my friend, reacted with catabolic energy. If the bride at the wedding screamed and threw a tantrum when her cake hit the floor (aka, reacting), the guests would probably feel uncomfortable and leave the reception early. Later, once she was able to process all the information, she may have felt guilt or experienced shame for her actions.

In contrast, when we respond thoughtfully, we create better outcomes. We can defuse tense situations, build healthier relationships, and make choices that align with our long-term goals. Responding empowers us to navigate unexpected turns with greater wisdom and grace. It's what allowed the bride to laugh it off and turn the potential disaster into a shared memory of joy.

Who we are in life is determined by our actions, which are entirely determined by our ability to respond rather than react to the cake on the floor. Whether we like it or not, when we die, we will leave behind a legacy. It's your impact on the world, the difference you made during your life, the things you've left behind. Every day, with every action you take, you create your legacy. The question is, are you creating your legacy by design or by default (responding or reacting)?

Problem Solved!

Great! All we need to do is learn how to respond in these situations instead of reacting, and then we can all ride off into the sunset, leading peaceful lives free of stress or worry. So why don't we? If responding gives us so much freedom and peace, why don't we always respond? In short, because we don't give ourselves time to do so.

To respond, we have to pause long enough to be aware that responding is even an option. Pausing isn't always easy in the middle of challenging situations, but it is essential to take conscious control of your life.

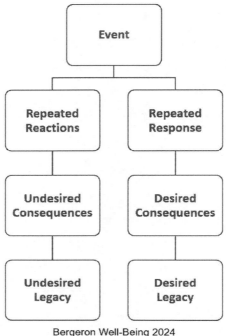

Bergeron Well-Being 2024

The Power of the Pause

Growing up in the 1980s, before computers became commonplace, I loved to read. One of my favorite types of books was "Choose Your Own Adventure." In these books, you decide what the characters will do next by turning to specific pages.

There would be an exciting cliffhanger scenario like "What does ingenue Jane Doe do when she hears a knock at the door while investigating the abandoned mansion at night during a thunderstorm?" As a reader, you could then decide what happened next. At the bottom of the page were options like:

Open the door slowly *(turn to page x)*

Turn off the lights and pretend no one is home (*Turn to page b)*

It was a fun and exciting way to be involved in the story. Some outcomes were better than others, but you never really knew until you made your choice and turned to the appropriate page. Sometimes, it took me several minutes to make a decision. Since it was a book, I had the ability to pause as long as I wanted before deciding. In real life, pausing is much more challenging.

A critical aspect of learning to respond is to develop awareness by recognizing the pause—the space between stimulus and reaction. In this pause, you have the opportunity to choose how you respond to unexpected situations.

Imagine you're in a heated argument with a loved one. During the conflict, you may notice a pause—a moment where you can choose to react with anger and defensiveness or respond with empathy and understanding. It's that moment of stillness where you gain control over your reactions and access the space for thoughtful responses. You get to *decide* what to do next.

"Between stimulus and response, there is a space. In that space is our power to choose our response. In our response lies our growth and our freedom."
Viktor E. Frankl

The pause is your ally, and it becomes more accessible with practice. Without practice, the pause can feel impossible to find. Think about the pause, like getting in shape. If you went to the gym one time, came home, looked at yourself in the mirror, and said, "Well, that didn't do anything," you're missing the point. You'll never make progress, you'll stop going, and you won't get results. It's a self-fulfilling prophecy.

The results become increasingly evident when you make it a ritual and intentionally stick with a wellness program. The same goes for learning how to pause. The more you do it, the better you get at creating that space between stimulus and reaction. What once may have taken you weeks to work through may now only take a moment.

CHAPTER 3 REFLECTION QUESTIONS

Understanding Reacting vs. Responding:
Think of a recent situation where you reacted automatically. What was the outcome, and how might the situation have differed if you had taken a moment to respond thoughtfully instead?

Identifying Catabolic Reactions:
Can you identify a scenario where your reaction was more catabolic, driven by stress or fear? How did this reaction affect your physical and emotional well-being?

The Significance of the Pause:
Reflect on a moment of conflict or stress. Did you notice a pause before reacting? If not, how might recognizing and utilizing this pause change your approach to similar situations in the future?

Practicing Response Over Reaction:
Consider a recurring stressor in your life. How can you prepare yourself to respond rather than react to this situation moving forward?

Learning from the Power of Choice:
When faced with a decision, how often do you consciously consider your options? How can you cultivate

a habit of pausing to choose your adventure more thoughtfully?

Growth from Adversity:

Recall a time when an unexpected challenge (your "cake on the floor" moment) led to personal growth or a positive outcome you hadn't anticipated. What did you learn about yourself through that experience?

Evaluating the Cost of Reacting:

Looking back, can you quantify what reacting impulsively has cost you in terms of relationships, opportunities, or peace of mind? How does this realization impact your perspective on responding vs. reacting?

The Role of Awareness:

How aware are you in moments of stress or conflict of the choice to react or respond? What strategies can you implement to enhance this awareness?

Creating Your Legacy:

Reflecting on the concept of legacy, how do your reactions and responses to life's challenges contribute to the legacy you wish to leave? Are you crafting this legacy by design or by default?

Overcoming Barriers to Responding:

What barriers prevent you from taking a pause and choosing to respond thoughtfully in stressful situations? How can you work to overcome these obstacles?

CHAPTER 4

SELF-AWARENESS

"THE MOST DIFFICULT THING IN LIFE IS TO KNOW YOURSELF."

— THALES OF MILETUS

A Few Tips

Before we dive into self-awareness, I want to take a moment to prepare you for what's coming. True self-awareness can be very uncomfortable. You've spent your entire life with a specific understanding of who you think and feel that you are. If you really want to get the most out of this book, some of the concepts and questions I raise in this section may cause you some discomfort. When you read something that you feel a reaction to, I encourage you to pause for a moment to explore what is really going on within you.

I realize this is quite the 'chicken and the egg' scenario in that I have not yet provided tools to help you learn how to strengthen and increase that pause. However, I feel it is important to provide the information and framework to understand your emotions and thoughts so that when I introduce helpful tools to create space in the later chapters, you will know what to seek and observe while creating space.

Tip 1: Instead of Self-Improvement, Focus on Self-Compassion

If you find resistance to certain concepts or ideas, don't shame yourself for feeling that resistance. You cannot bully yourself into growth and acceptance. There is nothing wrong with you. Let me repeat this. *There is nothing wrong with you. At all.* Don't judge yourself for how you feel or for not knowing something. View your triggers and reactions with curiosity, not contempt.

Wherever you are on your emotional, intellectual, and spiritual journey is perfectly fine. You feel how you feel. It will *always* be ok to feel how you feel. There is nothing wrong with your feelings. It's okay if you've never slowed down enough to process your feelings and thoughts, and it's perfectly okay if you do not consider yourself spiritual. It's taken me years… decades of therapy, journaling, meditation, support groups, plant medicine, and general life experience to allow me to *begin* accepting and loving myself.

When we shame ourselves for having a reaction, it creates more shame. The hardest line you will ever walk is the one between accountability and grace. As you start your journey of self-discovery, I encourage you to show yourself an abundance of grace. Be kind to all parts of yourself.

Tip 2: Journal it Out

If you experience resistance to a concept, ask yourself what you may be feeling or thinking. What could be the cause of it? Consider journaling what comes up for you as you begin to explore your feelings and thoughts. While you journal, do what you can to separate the facts from the judgments.

Tip 3: The Power of the Pause

It's okay to put this book down and come back to it later if something is particularly triggering. But I encourage you to return to it as soon as you can. Only by questioning how we feel and think we gain awareness of it. The Poet/Philosopher Rumi once said, "If you are irritated by every rub, how will you ever be polished?" Awareness of your triggers and their root causes is the only way to shift your perspective and achieve growth.

Tip 4: There is Always Cake on the Floor

It may be helpful to view anything you read that triggers you as cake on the floor. Ignoring it doesn't clean it up.

Acknowledging its existence and accepting there will always be cake on the floor allows you to work through it.

With this in mind, let's begin our exploration of self-awareness.

<u>Just Who Do You Think You Are?</u>

When you think of the term self-awareness, what comes to mind? On the surface, it may seem basic. When you ask yourself who you are, your name and profession are usually the first things that spring to mind.

True self-awareness is a deeper understanding of who you are beneath the labels. It's awareness of why you react to situations the way that you do. It's the comprehensive knowledge of your values, goals, triggers, emotions, thoughts, and purpose. Dr Tasha Eurich, an organizational psychologist and author of Insight: The Surprising Truth About How Others See Us, How We See Ourselves, and Why the Answers Matter More Than We Think, uncovered something remarkable in her research. Even though 95% of people believe they are self-aware, only 10-15% of people actually are.

<u>The 'Easy' Race</u>

For over a decade, I had a successful personal training business. I enjoyed helping my clients find goals that would challenge and motivate them. I remember helping a client, Joey, train for his first triathlon. Over a few months, he lost 40 lbs. and learned to swim. On race morning, he had the all-too-familiar feelings of nervousness, fear, and excitement. I helped him rack his bike in the transition area, and we reviewed his race plan. The longer we talked, the more I could see the confidence returning to his face.

As we were wrapping up our conversation, I noticed a more seasoned triathlete, Linda, whom I happened to know, walking through the sprint transition area with several of her seasoned triathlete friends in tow. There were two races that day: the sprint my client was doing and a much longer Olympic distance she had signed up for. As she realized she was standing in the middle of the sprint transition area, she very loudly proclaimed to her friends (and all within earshot), "Oh, I'm in the wrong place. This is the EASY race."

My blood boiled. Who does she think she is? She didn't know these people's stories. This wasn't easy for Joey. He was terrified. Another person I knew, Stacy, who had just beat cancer and was doing this sprint as her first triathlon ever as well! My mind was off to the races, and in my head, I was calling Linda every name in the book.

My lack of self-awareness blinded me from seeing how judgmental I was being. I was judging Linda just as much (if not more) than she was judging the athletes doing the shorter race. Her comments triggered an insecurity within me, and I was reacting emotionally. It made me feel self-righteous to condemn her in my mind. When in reality, all it did was cause *me* suffering and didn't affect her at all.

My anger and frustration were obvious to those around me. I mumbled about her under my breath, and my energy completely shifted from being there for Joey to ruminating on

Linda. I wasn't able to be there for Joey and help him get his mind ready for the race because my mind was filled with catabolic energy. In retrospect, I probably made Joey even more nervous about the race. My knee-jerk emotional reaction clouded my self-awareness. If I had taken a moment to pause and ask myself how I wanted to respond, I would have responded very differently.

Consider a scenario where a colleague criticizes your work during a team meeting. Your immediate reaction might be defensiveness, anger, or embarrassment. Without self-awareness, you might blindly follow these emotions, reacting defensively or perhaps lashing out in frustration.

However, with self-awareness, you can pause and examine your emotional reactions. You might realize that criticism triggers a deep-seated fear of inadequacy or a need for approval. This awareness provides a moment of choice—a choice to respond with composure and curiosity rather than reacting emotionally. Understanding one-off reactions is important, but to move towards greater self-awareness, you'll need to understand the full story you have written about yourself.

"The Story of My Life"

Ted was a new client of mine who felt very unappreciated. Eight months prior, he was brought in to be a Regional Vice

President of Operations for a medium-sized chain of family-owned restaurants. However, one of the locations in his region was without a general manager, so for the past six of those eight months, he has served in that capacity while still carrying out his duties as a VP. He was so buried managing that one restaurant, he hadn't had time to do any of the duties he was hired for. When I asked him why he was the one who had to fill the role, he said that the owners asked him to do it, so he agreed, not realizing the search would drag on for over half a year.

He also shared that his nephew, in his mid-thirties and wanting a change of scenery, decided to move to San Diego, where Ted lived. After coming to an agreement on rent and responsibilities, he moved in with Ted. For the past several months, his nephew always seemed to have emergencies pop up and was unable to contribute to the rent. Ted shared that this made him resentful since he had to make up the difference. "It would be different if he were cleaning up the place or cooking," he stated in a very defeated tone.

"I can see how that could be frustrating for you," I said empathetically. "It sounds like you sacrifice a lot to help other people."

His eyes widened, and he nodded emphatically. "Story of my life." He replied.

"What if it wasn't?" I asked.

I, once again, stared at the silent, introspective face of a client who had never thought to question their own story.

So, let's shift to you for a moment. If you, the person reading this book right now, had a movie being made about your life, who would play you in the starring role? What would you base your selection on? How much they looked like you? Your mannerisms? Who you wish you looked like?

Pause

Now that you have this person in mind, pretend you're a consultant on the set of this movie about your life. The script is mostly improv, and it's your job before every scene to tell this actor how to "be you" in the current predicament. How would you tell them to handle the scene where you got laid off from work? Or the one where your significant other starts yelling at your character, what should your character do to authentically "be you?" What about when your wedding cake came crashing down at your feet?

Let's say, halfway through filming, the director walks up and asks you if you felt this film about your life should be a romantic comedy, a tragedy, or an inspirational underdog

story. How would you answer? Up until now, you thought it was one type of movie, but maybe now you're not so sure. How would the ending be different if it was a thriller?

Well, guess what? Whether you like it or not, there is a movie being made about your life. Starring you. And you are the one writing, starring, and directing it every single moment. So what is the story you are telling yourself about your life? Do you like the story? No? That's okay. What is the story you *want* to tell?

After working with Ted for a few sessions, he began rewriting his story. Instead of feeling like he was stuck as a general manager, he decided to take the initiative. If the owners weren't going to hire a general manager, he was. He was a VP, after all! He was so used to playing the role of the victim that he hadn't considered he could also be his own savior. Within a few weeks, he found the perfect candidate and was able to resume his role in the corporate office full-time.

It's not easy to rewrite the story when you have been playing a role for so long. There are still plenty of times when Ted puts himself back into the victim role because, even though he doesn't like it, it's familiar to him. He didn't realize he had made it a part of his identity. It was difficult for him to set and stick with a boundary with his nephew, and he learned that was okay. He is changing the narrative and focusing on compassion for himself as he gets used to how it feels to set and maintain healthy boundaries. He is aware of old habits creeping back in and does what he can to reframe the situation and be honest with himself about his intentions.

Self-awareness is knowing the story, the role you are playing, and what goes into how you chose them. Because trust me, conscious or otherwise, you are choosing the story and the roles you play in your life. Writing our story is how we filter all the facts, judgments, and circumstances through our emotions and thoughts. It took me decades to gain enough awareness to rewrite the story of my life.

My Origin Story

Growing up, I faced a lot of challenges. I won't say that I had it better or worse than anyone; I can only say that I had a unique set of experiences that caused me to view the world differently. My father, an American, and my mother, a Palestinian, met and married while working overseas for the United Nations.

As a member of the UN, my father had diplomatic immunity and often did as he pleased, including how he treated my mother, brother, and me. He was a narcissist in the truest sense of the word, not in the "My ex was mean to me, so he is a narcissist" way the term tends to get slung around today.

My parents had separate bedrooms for as long as I could remember, and I don't recall a single instance of love, affection, or even kindness from my father towards my mother. Having many demons of his own, he would often act in cruel ways to show his displeasure. As is typical with traumatic childhoods, I only recall fragments, but I do recall a specific instance when I was around four years old.

My father had a few business associates over to our house in Aman, Jordan. He asked me to bring him a diet soda. Inadvertently, as a four-year-old, I brought him a regular one.

He called me over to him, pulled out the front of my pants, underwear and all, and proceeded to pour the soda down my pants in front of his guests. I don't remember the reaction of the other men in the room. But I can still feel the shock in my system and having to scoop the ice out of my underwear.

My father retired a little more than a year later when his physical health started to deteriorate as rapidly as his mental health. We moved from Geneva, Switzerland, to his hometown of Jonesboro, Arkansas. Growing up as a half-Arab in Arkansas, I was called every racist name in the book. My father, born in the rural south in 1932, also had very racist tendencies and was extremely vocal about friends I had of other races. He even made racist statements about my mother in front of my brother and me.

The only words I can still hear my father saying to me came when I asked him if I should be scared of God.

"Well, are you scared of me?"

The truth is, I wasn't just afraid of my father, I was terrified of him. I vaguely I remember saying no, that I wasn't scared, thinking that that was the right answer. Because the truth was irrelevant in any interaction with my father. To avoid punishment or embarrassment, I had to try and think three steps ahead and give him the answer I thought he wanted to hear.

On this occasion, I guessed incorrectly. I can't remember his exact reply, but the feeling of an 8-year-old's panic for picking incorrectly in that moment is still seared in my subconscious. I remember that bothering him because my father wanted me to be afraid of him. In his warped mind, fear meant respect.

It didn't dawn on me until recently how much his answer impacted my views of religion and spirituality. His self-aggrandizing analogy meant that God wasn't a benevolent Force existing within me and filling me with love. God was vengeful. God would pour a Coke down the pants of his four-year-old son in front of house guests because the son accidentally brought it to Him instead of a Diet Coke. God would never tell me he loved me. Nothing I ever did would be good enough for God.

As his diabetes grew worse, my father was no longer able to abuse us physically, but we often found ourselves walking on eggshells to avoid his emotional cruelty. His temperament was volatile, and my brother and I never knew what would set him off. He had both feet amputated from gangrene and, most nights, would moan and wail in pain.

By the time I was ten, he had also gone blind, and my brother and I found ourselves to be his caretakers while our mother worked. We had intercoms in our house that he would use to alert us when he was in need by rapidly pushing the page button. No matter what my brother and I were doing when we heard the beeps, we had to drop everything and attend to his every need, from bringing him water to helping him to the bathroom. When he became too weak to push the button, he transitioned to locking the intercom 'on' so we could hear every moan and scream everywhere in the house. We existed only to take care of his needs.

On January 14th, 1992, when my cousin came to our house to tell me my father died at the hospital, I remember feeling free for the first time in my life. Like the eggshells I had been walking on for all of my childhood has finally been swept away leaving bare earth where grass could once again grow beneath my feet. But my relationship with spirituality remained the same.

My mother, not believing in therapy, never had my brother or me get any counseling. We did our best to "suck it up" as we both developed unhealthy coping mechanisms to get us through life. It took nearly 30 more years before I did enough digging to find the origins of my dysfunction.

For most of my life, I hated my father. I hated who he was and what he did to me. But now, finding my real connection with my purpose and my higher power, I can forgive him. I can hate the sin but love the sinner. Because holding on to hate only validated how I felt about God. It was a self-inflicted wound based on a flawed value system uploaded to an 8-year-old.

The Aftermath

For many decades, I cast myself in the roles I thought I was supposed to play. Some were seemingly noble, such as the role of the underdog, dedicating my life to physical fitness. I was not going to die early like my father. I may be predisposed to diabetes, but I was not going to let it conquer me! I went on to become a spokesperson for a national supplement brand, and my slogan was "Don't be a prisoner of your genetics."

Deep below the surface of my conscious mind, I took on the role of victim. I never understood or set boundaries, always people-pleasing, especially to "grown-ups" or authority figures. This can be a dangerous role for anyone, especially a child. I found myself the victim of a predatory teacher in high school who sensed this energy and attempted to groom me for an inappropriate relationship. Being too scared to tell anyone or set a boundary, I carried the shame I felt into my forties when I was finally able to process my feelings by opening up about the experience and calling him out for the predator he was.

Confusing judgments for facts, I took on the role of the savior. I often found myself in relationships where I felt the other person needed me to help them. "Write what you know," they say. The script I wrote recreated the familiar feelings I had as a child that no one cared about how I felt or what my needs were. I bounced from toxic relationship to toxic relationship, always feeling like a victim when they cheated on me, left me, or no longer needed me. "Of course," I would tell myself. "This is the story of my life," completely unaware that I was the one writing it.

My story consisted of several elements that did not serve me:

- Unconsciously creating situations seeking the familiar yet uncomfortable emotions of my childhood.
- Believing the judgment that I was not as worthy as others because being an Arab meant I was bad.
- Blindly following authority figures because they are the grown-ups and I am not. (This would continue even when I was an adult).

All of these realizations have been very hard pills for me to swallow. Like I said at the beginning of this cha pter, true self-awareness can be very uncomfortable. But knowing *why* we write the stories we write is only part of the equation. We also need to know what to do when we become aware of the story to be able to change the script. And that involves understanding the role of emotions and thoughts operating below our conscious mind.

CHAPTER 4 REFLECTION QUESTIONS

Identifying Your Roles:

What roles have you found yourself playing in your life (e.g., the victim, the savior, the underdog)? How have these roles shaped your experiences and relationships?

Understanding Your Story:

Reflect on the origin of your current life story. How have your upbringing and significant life events influenced the narrative you've lived by?

Examining Your Choices:

In what ways have you been choosing, consciously or unconsciously, the story and roles you play in your life? Can you identify moments where a different choice could have led to a different path?

Breaking Free from Familiar Patterns:

What familiar but unhelpful patterns do you recognize in your life? How do these patterns serve you, and what fears might be holding you back from breaking free from them?

Setting and Respecting Boundaries:

How comfortable are you with setting boundaries? Can you recall a time when setting a boundary significantly impacted your well-being or relationships? What boundaries do you need to establish or reinforce in your life?

Embracing Self-Compassion:

How do you practice self-compassion, especially when confronting parts of your story you wish to change? How can you be kinder to yourself in moments of self-doubt or when old habits resurface?

Rewriting Your Narrative:

If you could start rewriting the story of your life today, what would you change? What new roles would you like to adopt, and what values or dreams would guide your new narrative?

Exploring Underlying Emotions and Beliefs:

What underlying emotions and beliefs have been driving your behaviors and choices? Are there any that no longer serve you, and how can you begin to challenge and change them?

The Power of Agency:

How do you perceive your own agency in changing your life story? What steps can you take to feel more empowered and proactive in creating the life you desire?

Envisioning Your Future:

Imagine your life several years from now, having successfully rewritten your story. What does this life look like? How do you feel, and what kinds of relationships and activities fill your days?

CHAPTER 5

EMOTIONS

"UNEXPRESSED EMOTIONS NEVER DIE. THEY ARE BURIED
ALIVE AND WILL COME FORTH LATER IN UGLIER WAYS.

— SIGMUND FREUD

Emotions play a central role in how we act in unexpected situations. To completely cover every nuance of the importance of emotions would take an entire library, so this chapter is by no means exhaustive. I focused the information to help you gain awareness of the role emotions play in our reactions and develop a foundation of emotional intelligence.

Emotional intelligence (also known as Emotional Quotient or "EQ") is the ability to understand, use, and manage your emotions as well as understand the emotions of others. How important is EQ? Study after study has shown that EQ has a four times greater impact on your success than IQ.

- According to the Center for Creative Leadership, "75% of careers are derailed for reasons related to emotional competencies, including inability to handle interpersonal problems; unsatisfactory team leadership during times of difficulty or conflict; or inability to adapt to change or elicit trust."
- 71% of Employers Say They Value Emotional Intelligence Over IQ" -Career Builder Jan 2023
- People with high emotional intelligence make an average of $29,000 per year more than people with low EQ. On average, every point increase in emotional intelligence adds $1,300 to an annual salary. - TalentSmart 2023
- A 40-year longitudinal investigation of 450 boys found that IQ had little relation to life success. The most significant predictors were handling frustration, controlling emotions, and getting along with others.

Sweet Emotion

So now that we know having greater emotional intelligence is paramount to success, the next step is figuring out... what is an emotion?

Let's start by identifying what an emotion is NOT: you. You are not your emotions. You are the one feeling your emotions. I'm not angry. I'm Ramsey. I feel anger. When we decide to identify and label ourselves as the emotion by saying something like "I am angry," we give up our power and let that emotion rule us. Creating space between ourselves and the emotion allows us to see we are the ones who are experiencing the emotion and not the emotion itself.

So, what is this thing that we call an emotion? In short, an emotion is a complex experience of consciousness, bodily sensation, and behavior that reflects the personal significance of a thing, an event, or a state of affairs. The key phrase to understand from this definition is "personal significance." What does the "thing" mean to you, whether it's a person, place, event, or memory?

Let's say you and two friends are walking down the street. Suddenly, up ahead, you notice someone is walking their dog, heading right toward you. Depending on the personal significance the person or the dog might have to you, all three of you could have very different emotional reactions.

One of you could feel scared, another excited, and one indifferent, based on one or several of the following conditions:
- Owning a dog of your own
- Your dog recently passed away
- Being bitten by a dog as a child
- Knowing this particular dog (or owner)
- The breed of the dog
- Is the dog wagging its tail or growling

It would take many pages to list the thousands of variables that contribute to the personal significance of this event, but you get the idea.

This same framework applies to every single thing you encounter in your life. Let's look at some possible factors that could influence the personal significance of your wedding cake falling on the floor:

- Other cake cuttings you have witnessed
- How much you like cake
- How much you paid for the cake
- How hungry you are
- How formal your family and culture are
- Your specific expectations of your wedding
- The strength of the relationship with your new spouse

Again, the list of variables could go on and on.

So, what does this mean regarding our reactivity? Often, *our emotional reaction is not about this event; it's about the original experience that happened to us that was subconsciously triggered by similar factors in the present, creating a subjective experience.*

This is why your early childhood is so influential on how you see the world as an adult. It's because that's when you experience most situations for the first time. Studies show that

50% of our subconscious programming is in place by the time we are seven years old.

Let's say you were five years old and got to play with a dog for the first time. That dog bit you, leaving a scar on your hand. At the time, that was a new, novel situation. Your mind then writes a story it thinks will help you in the future. In this scenario, the story may be "dogs are bad."

At an early age, we generally don't have much reasoning power, so unless we reprocess events like this as adults, the unresolved emotional impact of these events unconsciously colors our emotional responses for the rest of our lives. So now, without even thinking about it, you are triggered every time you see a dog. Your heart may start racing, and you may feel a heightened sense of anxiety, even if, on the surface, you know that chihuahua doesn't have the ability to do any significant damage to you. So even though the dog approaching you and your friends on the street is friendly, well-trained, on a leash, and wagging its tail, you are still unconsciously reacting based on what happened to you as a child.

Often, we will then do things that reinforce our initial belief and strengthen the personal significance of the thing. Maybe, when you see the dog, you jump back suddenly, and the dog, unaware of your intentions, thinks you are playing, so it jumps towards you. You may interpret that as aggression and tell yourself that the dog surely would have bitten you if you had not jumped back. This reinforces the initial story you tell yourself, and either consciously or subconsciously, you use it as evidence that your emotional response is fact-based and accurate even though it is not. This can leave us in a state of a catabolic reaction to situations based on personal significance that does not entirely mirror the reality of the current situation.

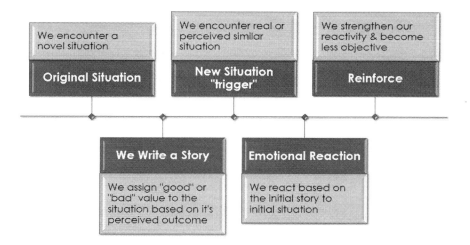

These triggers can also elicit "positive" emotional reactions! If your family owned a dog when you were young and your initial interactions were full of love and affection, you may feel drawn to dogs when you see them as an adult.

As a child, I had a Cocker Spaniel named Fancy that I loved very much. Now, whenever I take my dogs to the dog park, I usually remember the other dogs' names well before I remember the owner's.

I use this analogy about a dog because it's rather extreme. These emotional anchors are usually a lot subtler and subconsciously happen hundreds if not thousands of times a day. Smells, tastes, sounds (especially music!), people, weather, places, gifts, jokes, or even a single word can all hold personal significance that colors your current perspective of a situation.

Amanda, a coaching client of mine, was a mid-level executive who was struggling with how to deal with a male coworker, Larry. Standing over 6'4", Larry was a large, imposing man who would go out of his way to help anyone. He was a gentle giant. He also happened to be very passionate and had no qualms about sharing his strong opinions.

While passing each other in the hallways or at functions outside the office, Amanda and Larry got along very well. But in meetings, it was a very different story. Larry, with his larger-than-life personality, wanted his voice to be heard. Amanda described him as "going on the attack" and "explosive." Having consulted for this company for several years, I knew Larry rather well and knew his bark was much worse than his bite (apologies for another dog analogy so soon). Amanda knew it as well and that he wasn't being hostile toward her, but when he raised his voice in meetings, her heart would start racing, she wasn't able to think clearly, and would occasionally find herself on the edge of tears.

We dove into the root of her reaction, and after some exploration, I sensed the root of her feelings was not related to Larry at all. Having worked with her for a few months, I felt comfortable asking her, "Tell me about another time in your life when you felt unheard or dismissed by a large man."

A lightbulb went off for her. "Oh my God," she said. "I haven't thought about that in such a long time." It clicked for her that Larry was reminding her of a situation she was in as a teenager where she felt unheard and powerless. With this newfound awareness, we worked together to find ways for her to calm herself in meetings, and she strengthened her working relationship with Larry.

Naming the Feeling

What would you say if I asked you how you felt right now? Good? Bad? (Ironically, neither of these words are actually emotions.) One of the first things I do with a new client is provide them with a feelings wheel to help them learn how to name their feelings.* Having clarity and articulating what you are feeling goes a long way to help you work through the trigger and release the emotion. There is a significant difference between feeling humiliated and feeling jealous. If you stop at telling yourself you are angry and don't dial down

---

The Feelings Wheel was first developed by Dr. Gloria Willcox in 1982.

and find the root emotion, you won't be able to effectively work through it.

Feelings Wheel

<u>The Good, the Bad, and the Neutral</u>

One of the most insightful parts of my emotional mastery workshops is having the participants list all the emotions they have felt in the past month. Once they have the emotions written, I ask them to divide them into three columns: Good, Neutral, and Bad. Then, I ask for a volunteer to come forward so we can discuss the emotions they listed. We go down their list and address the emotions one by one.

For example, let's say they have "frustration" listed under the "Bad" column. I ask them if they could think of any scenario at all, whether they had been in that situation before or not, where frustration could be beneficial. Before you read ahead, pause for a moment (which will be good practice for pausing anyway) and ask yourself the same question: Can you think of any scenario where feeling frustrated may be beneficial?

… go ahead, I'll wait…

pause

If you think about it, there are probably several examples in which frustration can be beneficial. Being frustrated with a problem at work can motivate you to think outside the box to find new solutions. Frustration in a relationship can motivate you to explore what needs to change to find peace or reinforce boundaries that are being violated. In essence, frustration can motivate you to take action to make a change in your life. Now, it's true that excessive or extended frustration can definitely have negative consequences, but not every single time.

Next, I discuss the possible benefits of frustration, and then generally, the audience agrees that it should be labeled as a neutral emotion instead of a negative one. But I don't stop there. I do the same for the feelings in the "good" column. Let's say they listed "confident." Can you think of a scenario, whether you have personally experienced it or not, where someone feels so confident that it could be detrimental? Same drill… pause and reflect for a moment.

I can think of plenty of real-life examples where overconfidence led to "negative" consequences. Everything from risky financial investments to reckless driving, neglecting preparation for important events, ignoring expert advice, and much more can be attributed to being overconfident. After agreeing, we move confidence from the "good" column to the neutral one.

We do this for every emotion on the list, and by the end of the exercise, we realize that… all feelings are neutral. (insert mic drop here)

Yes. Every single emotion is inherently neutral.*

If you can wrap your head around this concept alone, you will free yourself from 90% of the needless suffering you experience in your life. We spend so much energy trying not to feel "bad" emotions that we don't listen to the message it is trying to relay. Especially if the message is *not even about this*

---

* The two exceptions to commonly listed emotions are "shame" and "gratitude," which I argue are mindsets more than they are emotions. Shame is a combination of several emotions that culminate in an overall sense of "I am less than" or "I am not good enough," where gratitude is a mindset comprised of seeking the good in situations even though "negative" emotions may be present.

scenario but about the original event that created the personal significance!

This is why emotional intelligence is so important. It allows us to name the emotion and understand that we are not the emotion. Instead of doing whatever we can to change our emotional state, we accept it and allow it to be. Feel your feelings, but don't become your feelings.

More Than a Feelin'

It's also important to realize that you can (and usually do) feel two or more conflicting emotions simultaneously. In 2019, I traveled to Ireland to compete in the inaugural Ironman Cork to make up for having dropped out of Ironman Norway the year prior.

Upon arrival in Ireland, I felt a sense of dread for the upcoming race. The forecast for the upcoming race day was a 100% chance of rain (welcome to Ireland!), my back was sore, and the water temperature for the ocean swim was a brisk 55 degrees Fahrenheit. When the race morning rolled around, I decided not to compete and felt a great sense of relief. Simultaneously, I felt disappointed that I had traveled all this way only to enjoy a Guinness while watching the rain fall through the pub window.

It is entirely possible to hold two feelings (like relief and disappointment) at the same time. Here are some situations that may elicit more than one emotion.

1) The Happiness and Sadness of Graduation

Earning your degree may bring you happiness as you begin your professional career and also sadness as you say goodbye to the friends and campus you are leaving behind.

2) The Excitement and Fear of Starting a New Job

You may experience excitement about the new opportunity and fear that you may not meet the expectations (damn you, expectations!) of others and yourself.

3) The Love and Hate of Ending a Relationship

You may still love your partner and the memories you shared while also hating the circumstances that led to the breakup.

4) Relief and Guilt for a Loved One's Passing

You may feel relieved that their suffering is over and guilty for having the feeling of relief.

5) Secure and Restless in an Unfulfilling Job

Knowing that you have a steady paycheck does provide security, but the job doesn't challenge you, which makes you feel unfulfilled.

6) Hope and Despair of Starting a Family

If you are trying to conceive, you could be hopeful when you know you are ovulating, and also feel despair every month you are unsuccessful.

Being able to sit with and name the different emotions goes a long way toward understanding what is important to you and how the scenarios in your life impact you. If you can name, sit with, and work through your emotions, you will be well on your way to having a high EQ.

The Transient Nature of Feelings

It was a magical, star-studded night. My wife and I dressed to the nines, walking the red carpet outside Grohman's Chinese Theatre on Sunset Boulevard for the premiere of a movie I was in. Ever since I was a little this had been a dream of mine.

For a few short hours in 2018, that dream, nearly 40 years in the making, was a reality. I wasn't the star of the movie, not by a long shot. That was okay! There I was, a pivotal speaking part in two separate scenes. I finally felt the joy and pride I had sought for a lifetime. I didn't realize just how quickly that would change.

Two days later, driving home to Arizona, an emptiness grew inside me. It was uncomfortable, yet familiar. I told myself I shouldn't be feeling this way. I had just checked off a bucket list item! I had hoped for this moment my whole life! When I was seven, my younger brother and I would make our mom sit down to watch plays we wrote and starred in. The first time I could take acting classes in high school, I signed up.

Even though I was a chemical engineering major during my first semester of college, I auditioned and was cast as Tybalt in Romeo & Juliet, prompting me to change my major. I did community theater, got an agent, and started playing unpaid parts. I didn't care; I still wanted to do it and experience it. My first paying acting job was being Captain Morgan, going to bars, and handing out bottles of rum. Then, I got cast in smaller parts and worked my way up until I got a break. After years of auditions, rejections, rehearsals, and roles, I had made it to the red carpet.

Ok. Now what?

It was the same emptiness that followed the accomplishment I felt a few days after crossing an Ironman finish line. Different achievement, same outcome. After years of training, traveling, injuries, and inspiration, I had done it only to feel empty a short time later.

I started to analyze other areas of my life. Is this how I feel after every goal I set? Does that feeling of elation, triumph, pride, and perseverance fade? Yes. Every. Single. Time.

Feelings, like everything else in life, are impermanent. No feeling you have will last forever. Trying to have a feeling forever is like trying to nail down a wave at the beach to keep it from returning to the sea. For so many years, this caused me so much needless suffering. I would cross a finish line, feel incredible for a few days, then feel empty. I got married, and after the literal honeymoon period wore off, I felt like something was missing.

<u>Gooooooooaaaall…?</u>

There is a fallacy that most of us hold in regard to our expectations (damn you, expectations!) in relation to our goals and emotions. Let's look at a few goals you may have had in your life:

- Getting a promotion or starting your own company
- Moving to a new city
- Making more money
- Getting a new car/phone/house
- Getting married and/or having children
- Going on vacation and taking that perfect photo of a landmark

Now ask yourself, how long did the feeling of fulfillment last after you achieved it? Years? Months? Days? Some may be as fulfilling now as the day you accomplished it. Others, not so much. Why do you suppose that is? Would you believe me if I told you it was because the goal you were hoping to accomplish wasn't the real goal you were after? Let me explain.

Think about a goal you currently have in your life. It can be anything substantial. Close your eyes and really picture it.

Got it? Good.

Now, in a few words, describe how you will feel once you have achieved it. Again, close your eyes for a moment and really think about it. What feelings came up for you?

That feeling? The feeling you think you will have once you achieve your goal?

THAT is the real goal.

Let that sink in for a minute. Every meaningful goal or path you have pursued in your life was about the *feeling* you thought you would have when you accomplished it.

I wanted to walk the red carpet at a movie premiere because I wanted to *feel* like I was a successful actor. I wanted to do an Ironman because I wanted the *feeling* of accomplishment.

Many couples decide they want children. Without realizing it, many are often chasing the feeling of unconditional love and a sense of purpose. They think a child will give them that feeling. It's not the child, the red carpet, the job promotion, or finishing an Ironman that we really want. It's the feelings we believe accomplishing or acquiring those things will provide.

Even when the goal is financial, it's not about the money itself. It's the *feeling* of freedom you believe money will provide. You don't get a new car just because you want the car. It's often about how you think owning it will make you feel, how you think you will feel when others admire your purchase or see you driving in it. Maybe you link a particular car to your perception of success or to an image of who you want to be. Marketers are keenly aware of this. If you want others to see you as someone who can afford luxury, you may buy a Lexus or Mercedes. If you want others to see you as a rugged individualist, you may purchase a Jeep. It comes down to how you think you will feel wearing the role of "successful" or "rugged." The feeling you want to experience is paramount in that decision.

How many times have you bought something and, a short time later, thought, "Why the heck did I buy that?" It's because you're chasing feelings. You may think of yourself as logical, but we all make decisions emotionally and justify them rationally.

When I was a personal trainer, I had several clients who were very financially successful. Getting to know them over years of working together, I saw that some were more fulfilled than others. If you want to see how aware someone is that they are chasing feelings, watch how they spend their disposable income. One client may pull up in a different luxury car every week, and another client may show up to every session in a 10-year-old Civic, yet both are in the same tax bracket. In getting to know the former, it became clear that they kept getting new cars because they thought it would make them feel a certain way.

Bergeron Well-Being 2024

Few consider the emotions influencing a goal or decision before undertaking it. We think we want to accomplish that goal when, in reality, it's the *feeling* we believe we will experience when we achieve the goal, only to achieve it and discover just how impermanent feelings are.

That fulfillment won't last forever, yet we treat it like a box to be checked off. But that check was made in invisible ink, and before you know it, you have to move on to a new goal or action to experience that same impermanent feeling.

Now that you have a rudimentary understanding of your emotions, let's develop some awareness about our minds and how we think.

CHAPTER 5 REFLECTION QUESTIONS

Identifying Emotional Triggers:

Can you recall a recent situation where your emotional reaction surprised you? What do you think was the real trigger behind this reaction?

Reflect on a time when a seemingly minor event elicited a strong emotional response from you. What underlying memories or experiences might have influenced this response?

Understanding Personal Significance of Emotions:

Identify an object, smell, sound, or word that evokes a strong emotional response in you. What is the story or memory associated with it? How do these personal significances shape your perception of new experiences?

Exploring the Root of Your Feelings:

Think of an emotion you've recently felt but found difficult to explain. Can you identify any past experiences that might be influencing this feeling?

Have you ever noticed a pattern in your emotional responses that could be traced back to a particular event or series of events in your life?

Naming and Differentiating Your Emotions:

When you feel overwhelmed, can you take a moment to

identify and name the specific emotions you're experiencing? How might this practice change your approach to managing these feelings?

Can you distinguish between the surface emotion and the underlying root emotion in high-stress situations?

Reevaluating the Nature of Emotions:

Consider an emotion you typically categorize as "bad." Can you envision a scenario where this emotion might serve a beneficial purpose?

Reflect on an emotion you generally view as "good." Can you think of a situation where it might lead to negative outcomes?

Accepting the Duality of Feelings:

Can you identify a moment in your life where you experienced two conflicting emotions simultaneously? How did you navigate this complexity?

How does recognizing the possibility of holding multiple emotions at once change your understanding of your emotional responses?

The Transient Nature of Feelings:

Reflect on a time when you achieved a long-desired goal. How did your feelings change over time after achieving it?

How does acknowledging the impermanence of emotions affect your pursuit of happiness and fulfillment?

Goals and Emotional Fulfillment:

Think about a goal you have for yourself. Why is this goal important to you, and what emotions do you anticipate feeling once you achieve it?

Have you ever achieved a goal and then felt an unexpected emptiness afterward? What might this indicate about the nature of fulfillment and happiness in your life?

Chapter 6

Your Mind is (in) the Way

"The mind adapts and converts to its own purposes the obstacle to our acting. The impediment to action advances action. What stands in the way becomes the way."

— Marcus Aurelius

Having challenged myself physically most of my life, in August 2021, I decided to tackle a challenge that would test my mental limits: Ten days of silent meditation. Most people who knew me were skeptical that I could be quiet for ten minutes, let alone ten days. More than one of them told me I was crazy. Ten days of silent meditation taught me that we all are.

I was one of 40 students who drove across the desert to call the 154-acre Southern California Vipassana Center home for the next week and a half. Nestled up against Joshua Tree National Park, it was an unassuming compound built to blend into the surrounding desert. After some basic instructions from a facilitator, I turned over my keys and phone and began my 10-day silent meditation experience. There would be no talking, eye contact, exercise, music, writing, or reading for the duration. My life would consist of two meals and ten hours of meditation per day, all in an attempt to find tranquility and learn how to tame my restless mind.

For as much as we know about our mind, most of us still know nothing about its unconscious control over us. It's both our greatest obstacle and the means with which to conquer the same obstacle. During that retreat and in the years since, I learned a lot about my subconscious and the nature of thought. Much like in the earlier chapter on emotions, I won't be able to cover the entirety of such a deep subject, but to help set your expectations, I will do my best to share the parts I feel are relevant to the subject of this book.

Thought Neutrality

One of the first concepts I learned at the center was that thoughts, like emotions, are neutral. They are the automatic brainstorming sessions of our minds and are not inherently good or bad in themselves. We have the choice to judge our own thoughts as freely as we can judge outside events.

Think about it this way: you might see your dog napping on the couch and have a thought about going to pet your dog. That thought isn't good or bad; it's just an idea popping up in your head. Say you decide to act on it and walk over and gently pet your dog. You have taken that thought, found it worthy of actuating, and carried it out.

Now, let's flip the coin. Imagine you see your dog, and out of nowhere (which is where most thoughts originate from), the thought pops into your head, wondering what it would be like to punt your dog like a football across the living room. If this thought popped into your head, you may begin to feel like you are a terrible human being. After all, why on earth did a thought like that pop into your head? You may begin to spiral, wondering what is wrong with you. In reality, nothing is wrong with you. In reality, *thoughts think themselves.*

The thought itself isn't evil; it's just a thought. It just popped in there. You didn't try to think it. Now, if you decide to act on the thought, then yes, you have given power to that thought, and though thoughts are not good or bad, actions can be if they cause harm to you or others. Understanding this can help us be more aware of our inner world and make better choices in our actions. After all, it's our actions that define our moral compass, and thoughts are just thoughts.

The Observer, Not the Thinker

An important shift in perspective to help you take control of your mind is the awareness that you are the observer, not the thinker, of your thoughts. "You" are the consciousness that is aware that thoughts are taking place. Allow me to explain.

Let's use the earlier example of the intrusive thought that pops into your head to kick your dog. If you identify that it was you who thought it and what a "bad" thought it was, your inner monologue may continue, saying something like, "Oh my God, why did I think that? I am a TERRIBLE person for even thinking that thought." Here's the thing: *You* didn't actively think that thought. *You* are the person who is able to observe that thought and decide if you want to give it power or not. You are not the thinker; you are the observer. Remember, *thoughts think themselves.*

If you are someone who has identified with their thoughts and feelings all of your life, this can be a very challenging notion to wrap your head around. Fundamentally, I am asking you to question what you use to define who you are. This is the way to move from the 95% of people who think they are self-aware to being one of the 10-15% who actually are.

Tool: Giving Voice to the Thought

When to use it: *When you find yourself having an intrusive thought.*

Whenever you notice an intrusive thought, whether it is negative self-talk or a thought that is in some way suggesting an action or idea that is not in line with your values, try to give that "thought" a unique voice that is decidedly not your own. For example, when I have a thought that tells me I am not good enough or to do something out of character, I immediately use my imagination and put the thought in the voice of the late comedian and voice of the Aflac duck, Gilbert Gottfried. Placing the thought in his shrill, comical voice helps me see that I am not the thought and allows me to view it as separate from myself. This helps me detach and view it as a neutral observer.

The Restless Monkey Mind

Picture a mischievous monkey, agile and untamed, swinging from branch to branch in the heart of a dense forest. Its actions are ceaseless, marked by sudden jumps, incessant chatter, and a relentless search for the next destination. Now, imagine this monkey as a metaphor for your thoughts—an astute portrayal of the ever-active, ever-jumping nature of your mental processes.

Our minds often mirror this mischievous monkey, continuously leaping from one branch of thought to another without a moment's pause. These thoughts can be impulsive, unpredictable, and frenzied, dragging our consciousness along for the ride.

Think back to your morning commute or your last trip to the grocery store. If I were to ask you to describe that drive, would you be able to? Or was your monkey mind busy swinging from branch to branch? This could sound something like,

> *"Did my husband pick up the dry cleaning today? I wonder what we are going to do for dinner. I'm hungry; I wonder if I have time to hit up a drive-through on my way to work. I may not need to if Stephanie is bringing donuts in again. I'm still laughing at that joke Stephanie told me last week. What were her kids' names again? I think her son is named Trevor. I like the name Trevor..."*

and on and on—that nonstop, endless chatter accompanying us throughout our day. While our monkey mind is swinging from thought to thought, the one thing it tends not to focus on is the one thing we are doing—in this case, driving to work.

The Lost Present Moment

Consider being in the present moment during that commute or trip to the store —the windows down, the soft rustling of leaves in the breeze, the warmth of the sun on your skin, and the subtle rhythm of your breath as your hands gently grasp the wheel. This is the gift of the present, where life unfolds in its purest form.

An overactive monkey mind steals the richness of the present moment away from us. It distracts us from life's wonders and the simple joys that surround us. We become spectators of our own lives, unable to fully engage in the beauty and serenity of the here and now. When we are listening to the chatter of the monkey mind, we are always either in the future or the past and never in the present moment. The present moment is the only moment you will ever have control over.

In the moment after your wedding cake fell to the floor, you have no control over why it fell, how it fell, or how the venue plans on cleaning up the cake. It's just you, in that moment, with the cake. Thats it! So how do you choose to spend that moment? *Your actions at this moment are the only thing that will ever be in your control.*

By observing our thoughts without judgment and gently redirecting our wandering minds to the stillness of the present moment, we begin to tame this inner monkey. It's the realization that you are not the thinker. You are the observer of those thoughts. In other words, you are not the monkey; you are the person *watching* the monkey. This is an incredibly freeing notion!

Once you observe the monkey mind running rampant, you can consciously decide to return to the present moment. When the cake falls on the floor, the monkey mind may tell you that you should be upset! You spent a lot of money on that cake! But if you recognize you are the observer, you can decide how you want to respond. You can create space and determine that it doesn't matter if the cake is on the floor; you are still married, and you can have a food fight! Either way, the choice is yours *if* you create that magical pause to be able to enact it.

Habit Energy

While the monkey mind represents the restless nature of our thoughts, habit energy is the autopilot mode that often guides our actions, a pattern we follow without conscious awareness. It operates in the background, subtly influencing our decisions and reactions. This can be done intentionally when you practice a new skill or unintentionally when you mindlessly repeat certain behaviors.

Swimming did not come naturally to me. My first two triathlons were ocean swims, which felt like the opening scene of Saving Private Ryan. I was terrified. Loud noises and people screaming filled my ears when I came up for air, and I vomited when I stumbled out of the ocean onto the beach. So, I decided to teach myself how to swim. After spending hour after hour, day after day in the pool, after a few years, swimming became my favorite cardio activity. So much so that I was able to complete the 12.5-mile swim around Key West, Florida, without feeling like I was landing on the beaches of Normandy.

The way we get better at anything is through repetition. Doing something enough times means we do it without thinking, operating on autopilot. Imagine a well-trodden hiking trail through the woods. It is a groove in the terrain, formed by the footsteps of thousands of travelers who have walked the same route.

When I focused my effort on swimming so that the stroke became automatic, I was creating a similar well-worn path as an intentional habit (which I refer to as 'ritual"). Each swim session in the pool was my mind walking along that same path, strengthening that specific neural connection in my mind. This creates a deeply ingrained pattern of thoughts and behaviors. Swimming became second nature. It was intentional repetition. I no longer had to "think" about swimming. Now, when I get in the water, I can enjoy feeling the water against my skin and hearing the air leave my lungs without consciously thinking about my stroke or breathing.

This is great when we repeat behaviors intentionally. However, it can also lead us to develop bad habits when we repeat patterns of thoughts, actions, and reactions over and over without pausing to fully understand the consequences. This is referred to as habit energy.

When you wake up first thing in the morning, do you check your phone? Do you spend thirty minutes (or more) checking email, Facebook, Instagram, TikTok, and text messages before you get up? If so, is that what you *want* to do? Or is it just something you have done for so long it's automatic?

That's an example of habit energy. Mindlessly being drug along by your unconscious habits. By mindlessly grabbing your phone when you wake up day after day, month after month, year after year, you have worn a trail through the woods you did not intend to go down. Without thinking, you have allowed habit energy to dictate the course of your morning.

There is a zen saying about a man riding a horse that's galloping down the road at full speed. A passerby yells to the man, "Where are you going?"

He then replied, "I don't know. Ask the horse."

This horse is habit energy, and most of us allow it to direct where we go. We don't actively participate in our own lives.

The Impact of Habit Energy

Once our brain lays down and reinforces these paths, it can be really hard to find new ways to go. A better analogy is a river cutting through rock. Once a river has carved a deep path into rock, it becomes confined by its banks with no other way to go. Habitual reactions can become a prison, limiting our potential for personal growth and positive change. Our lives can become stagnant and repetitive when driven solely by these well-worn patterns. It hinders our ability to adapt to new circumstances, stifles creativity, and perpetuates stress and anxiety.

Other problematic ways that habit energy can manifest:

- Negative self-talk
- Unhealthy relationships
- Addictions
- Procrastination
- Comfort zones

Tool: Is This Serving Me?

When to use it: *When you want to gain awareness of your habit energy and change your patterns.*

As you go through your day, focus your awareness on your actions and determine if you are engaging in them out of habit energy. Some questions to ask yourself include:

1. Is this what I want to do be doing with my time right now?

2. How is this action serving me?

> *A. If this is not what I want to do with my time right now, what do I want to be doing instead?*
> *B. What ritual can I intentionally create to reinforce a new desired behavior or outcome?*

Our Ego and Ownership

If I were to ask you how you would have felt if you watched that cake fall to the floor, you might ask a fundamental follow-up question.: "As a guest or as the bride?"

Why should that make a difference? An important aspect of how we choose to act in situations is if we feel what is happening affects us personally. And according to our greedy little ego, that includes anything we *feel* we own. If it was OUR combination of sugar, flour, eggs, milk, and icing, then it's a tragedy. If it's someone else's? Not as much. It's still the exact same ingredients, just not the ones we feel belong to us.

I am intentionally saying the one you *feel* belongs to you because you will still have an emotional reaction even if you don't own the item in question, but you feel entitled to it.

Now This Takes the Cake

Let's say you've entered a raffle to win a wedding cake along with three hundred other people. You all file into the auditorium where the winner will be announced, and there, on stage, is the most beautiful wedding cake you have ever seen. A large banner adorns the back curtain of the stage where the words "This could be YOUR cake!" jump out in a dark red font across a white background. On the table next to the cake is the raffle ticket drum, slowly being rotated by the emcee. You watch all the tickets, including yours, tumble around, waiting for the hand of fate to select the winning one, hoping it's yours.

As you eagerly await the winning ticket to be drawn, you notice a man casually walking out from backstage toward the table. After doing a double take, you realize it's 90s prop comic Gallager, who happens to be carrying his patented sledge-o-matic sledgehammer.

Let's let this play out in the style of my favorite type of book growing up: a Choose Your Own Adventure book! (For those unfamiliar, turn to the corresponding page in this book to continue the story the way you want to experience it.)

> The emcee, in complete shock, doesn't have time to pull out the winning ticket before Gallager smashes the cake. *(turn to page 178)*

> The emcee draws the ticket, and you find out you won the cake before Gallager smashes it. *(turn to page 184)*

> The emcee draws the winning ticket belonging to a stranger, and then Gallager smashes the cake. *(turn to page 180)*

> The emcee draws the winning ticket belonging to Susan Spiteful, the person you dislike more than anyone else in the world, and then Gallager smashes the cake. *(turn to page 182)*

You exit the auditorium, and life goes on.

The variations of how the previous event could have played out illustrate that it's our attachment to things we feel we own, not the things themselves, that cause us suffering. This is where a slight shift in perspective can be so helpful.

Zero Our

In order to eliminate a lot of unnecessary suffering in your life, try viewing yourself as the caretaker instead of the owner of everything in your life. For some of you, this may be stepping into "woo woo" (hippie-dippie to the Lehman) territory. In my Radical Acceptance class, I discuss with my students what they own and what they feel that ownership means to them.

Let's say you're in my class, and I ask you what you own, and you tell me you own your house. Ok, well, let's say, hypothetically, your house catches on fire. Would you stand in front of the house and scream at the fire that it doesn't have the right to burn your home because you own it? How does *owning* it negate its inherent impermanence?

If you are in a car accident, and God forbid, to get you out of the car, they have to remove your badly mangled arm. Do you yell at the firemen and EMTs that they can't remove it because it's YOUR arm? "I don't know what to tell ya," they may reply, "It's the only way you're gonna live."

Owning something might be helpful regarding the laws of the state and country you live in, but how does that show up practically? Usually, a sense of owning something creates subconscious shifts in our mindset:

- We feel entitled to its guaranteed security and existence.
- We view it as an extension of ourselves.
- We fear it's destruction or someone else separating us from it.
- We feel a sense of loss when we no longer "own" it.
- We take it for granted and do not maintain or appreciate it.
- We need to own more because the sense of ego we have in what we own so far has faded, and we need more.

Viewing ourselves as a caretaker has very different implications. We know it won't be ours forever, so we do what we can to preserve it and respect it for as long as possible. When we are a caretaker, we:

- We treat it respectfully.
- We accept that it will inevitably break or be taken from us
- We are at peace when it changes form (i.e., gets destroyed, grows old, gets lost or stolen) because we realize it was never ours to begin with.
- We treat everything with respect because we recognize all things' inherent value and impermanence.

Back to Awareness

As you reflect on how your emotions and thoughts can prevent you from laughing at the cake on the floor, try not to allow that to overwhelm you. Don't judge yourself for your thoughts or feelings! It's about the awareness of what you are experiencing. After all, now that you are aware of them, you can begin to cultivate a practice to shift your perspective by creating space between your thoughts and emotions using the tools you will learn in the following chapters.

CHAPTER 6 REFLECTION QUESTIONS

Habit Formation and Rituals:

Reflect on a daily activity you perform automatically. How did this become a habit, and what does it say about your priorities and values?

Consider a skill or habit you've successfully cultivated through repetition. What steps did you take to make this behavior automatic, and how has it benefited you?

Identifying Habit Energy:

What are some examples of "habit energy" in your life that you've followed without intentional thought? How do these habits impact your daily life and overall well-being?

Can you identify a habit that you initially started with a positive intention but has now become an automatic behavior that may not serve you anymore? How can you begin to change this pattern?

Self-reflection on Habitual Responses:

Think of a recent situation where you reacted automatically, based on habit energy, rather than responding thoughtfully. What triggered this reaction, and how might you approach similar situations differently in the future?

How do your habitual responses to certain situations

confine or limit your potential for growth, creativity, or happiness?

Awareness and Change:

When you catch yourself engaging in an automatic behavior, ask yourself: "Is this action serving me?" Reflect on actions you've taken today that were more habit than choice. What would you like to change about these habits?

Consider an activity you perform mindlessly, such as checking your phone first thing in the morning. What intention could you set to replace this habit with something more meaningful or beneficial?

Ego and Ownership:

Reflect on something you own that you're particularly attached to. How does this attachment influence your emotions and behavior? How would your perspective change if you viewed yourself as a caretaker rather than an owner?

Think of a situation where you felt strong emotions due to a sense of ownership or entitlement. How did this affect your reaction, and what can this teach you about the nature of attachment and impermanence?

Shifting Perspectives:

In what ways do you allow "the horse" of habit energy to

dictate the direction of your life? What steps can you take to regain control and make more conscious choices? How can adopting the mindset of a caretaker over that of an owner reduce suffering and increase your appreciation and respect for the things and people in your life?

CHAPTER 7

MINDFULNESS

"FOR UNLESS ONE IS ABLE TO LIVE FULLY IN THE PRESENT, THE FUTURE IS A HOAX.

— ALAN WATTS

If I were to ask you about a superpower, what comes to mind? Maybe it's the ability to fly like Superman or strength like the Hulk. What probably didn't come to mind (no pun intended) is mindfulness. Yet, when you think of everything that mindfulness helps you accomplish, it truly is a real-life superpower.

In the last section of this book, I discussed several of the ways that our minds can be our own worst enemy. Mindfulness is the way to make peace with our mind. It allows us to be exactly who we want to be. To act in a way that is in alignment with our values, principles, goals, and purpose. How? By strengthening the pause, stopping the monkey mind, creating awareness of our thoughts and emotions, and breaking our habit energy.

As I dive into mindfulness, I'm going to ask for a bit of grace. I'm doing my best to encapsulate the essence of a subject that has been covered a thousand times by a thousand people. I've taken what I have learned from numerous sources and will try to explain it in a way that is easily digestible. I'm also going to reiterate that you may feel some resistance to concepts and parables I share. Your ability to connect to the content on mindfulness may depend on your current ability to be mindful. Keep an open mind, and if something doesn't resonate, that's okay. Keep what serves you and throw away what doesn't.

If what I share does resonate, it should give you an intellectual understanding of it. To truly *feel* its importance, it's up to you to move from that intellectual to an experiential understanding by applying it. For example, I can explain what it takes and how swimming 12.5 miles in the ocean will feel. But you can only truly know the experience when you dive in and swim it yourself.

Defining Mindfulness

Ok, great, so the answer to all of life's problems and embracing the cake on the floor is mindfulness. That raises another question: What *is* mindfulness? Other than the most overused word of the 21st century.

Pop quiz:

Which of these activities is the most mindful:

   A. Having dinner with your family
   B. Driving to work
   C. Meditating
   D. Talking with a coworker
   E. Reading a book about cake written by some guy you've never heard of

The answer? *Whichever you are doing at this moment* (Hopefully E).

Mindfulness is to be fully present in everything you are doing, fully aware of your thoughts and feelings, and not overly reactive to the things happening around you. It's being in the moment without judgment about the moment. That's how it allows you to create and strengthen the pause. Because if you are mindful, you are in the state of the eternal "now."

When you consider all the factors that prevent your awareness from being in the present moment, it's easy to see why being mindful is so important. Your reactions tend to stem from something that happened in the past or a worry that something may happen in the future. Neither of these is within your control if you are not focused on what is happening now.

Thich Nhat Hanh once said:

> *"If while washing dishes, we think only of the cup of tea that awaits us, thus hurrying to get the dishes out of the way as if they were a nuisance, then we are not 'washing the dishes to wash the dishes.' What's more, we are not alive during the time we are washing the dishes. In fact, we are completely incapable of realizing the miracle of life while standing at the sink. If we can't wash the dishes, the chances are we won't be able to drink our tea either. While drinking the cup of tea, we will only be thinking of other things, barely aware of the cup in our hands. Thus we are sucked away into the future—and we are incapable of actually living one minute of life."*

I had difficulty understanding exactly what he meant the first hundred times I read that. Let me see if I can break it down a little more simply. Why is being in the present moment so important? How does it allow you to realize the miracle of life?

For starters, it's the only time you have the power to observe the real world around you. Anything else is just a fantasy or a memory. It's also the only time in which you can actually do anything. Sure, you think you can do things in the future, but in reality, everything you have planned for the future can only be done when the future becomes "now."

A lot of the time, what happens is you spend "now" thinking about what you want to do or will do in the future. Guess what that leaves you doing right now? Nothing. You become paralyzed in the only moment in which you have the authority to take any action because you are daydreaming about what you will do when you get to a future moment. And guess what happens when we get to the future moment we were fantasizing about? You worry and stress about some *other* future moment and don't stay present in what is currently happening in *this* moment!

Being stuck regretting the past is just as unhelpful. Wishing the cake didn't fall to the floor doesn't go back in time and stop it from falling. But it does prevent you from accepting it and taking any action in this moment.

Wedding Presence

Let's look at mindfulness as it relates to our cake on the floor story as if you were the bride. Let's start at the beginning of the wedding day and see how it would progress with mindfulness. You will spend hours getting ready with your bridesmaids, getting dressed, and enjoying marrying the love of your life. Now, if you were worried something terrible might happen on your wedding day, you would be spending all of those moments worrying about what might go wrong and not focusing on the moment you are in! Instead of lip-singing your favorite song with your maid of honor while sipping champagne, you are worried about something that may or may not happen in the future, which you have no control over. You are not in the only moment you can enjoy: this one.

So, let's say you manage to stay fully present, enjoying those moments and every following moment as they arrive. You walk down the aisle, hold the hands of the man you are going to marry and feel him slip the ring on your finger. You look in his eyes, you say I do, and you are now pronounced husband and wife.

Then, at the reception, you enjoy your dinner, tasting every bite and being present with your husband and your guests. Then, you go to cut the cake and ... well, ya know.

As you are standing there and the cake is on the floor at your feet, what are you able to do in that moment to change the situation? Nothing. To be present in that moment is to be a witness to reality and accept the things that are happening. You can't go back and undo anything. Wondering what will happen after the reception ends doesn't help you right now, either.

Being present, you take in the scene with all of your senses, seeing the remnants of the cake on the floor, feeling the lack of resistance that now greets the end of your knife, hearing the collective gasp of air from your guests, and smelling the icing that still seems to hang in the air.

At this moment, if you are fully present, you get to decide how you want to interpret this and what you want to do *now*. Do you want to start a food fight with your husband and your guests and be playful in the moment? Do you want to laugh and ask the caterer if they have any more desserts they could possibly set out? Do you want to ask your maid of honor to run to Costco to pick up a delicious sheet cake?

By being present, you can create that magical pause and fully explore the options you have at this moment in reality. But only if you are able to combat your monkey mind and default emotional reaction to something unplanned that happened.

Monkey Mindfulness

Monkey Mind is great at getting you worked up long before there is ever a real issue. When I was a personal trainer, I would sometimes work from 5 am to 8 pm, training fourteen clients a day. I would wake up at 3:30 am, lamenting the day ahead. I knew it would *be* such a long day that I would already be aggravated by the time I was training my 7 am client. "Oh my God," I would think, "I can't believe I have to do this for twelve more hours. I'm *going to be* so exhausted."

I wasn't exhausted yet, mind you. My monkey mind was so upset that it was going to be a long day that I was not focusing on the only client I was able to help at that moment: the one right in front of me. I was 'pre-upset,' which made me actually upset and cranky long before my actual energy reserves were expended.

Can you relate to having so much to do in one day that you are stressed just thinking about it? It's mentally exhausting! So much so that you exhaust yourself mentally long before the reality of being exhausted physically. The fight or flight mode you put yourself in becomes so draining that it becomes a self-fulfilling prophecy, and you prematurely physically exhaust yourself.

Shed Your Shame and Then Reframe

Being fully present in every moment is not easy. Hell, I still have trouble doing it for extended periods of time. But it is something I strive to get better at every day. Early on, I would get so mad and shame myself when I noticed I wasn't being present. The negative voice in my head would call me stupid and tell me to give up. I'm an old dog, and I wasn't going to learn a new trick. What I didn't realize at the time was that noticing that I was not being present was actually the first step in being present!

Awareness that you are not being present allows you to bring your attention back to the present moment. If you never notice your lack of presence, then you can never return. Think of it this way: if you get lost while hiking in the woods, you cannot begin to find your way home until you realize you are lost.

Have you ever gotten in the car and started driving somewhere, and several minutes later, you realized you were not driving toward your intended destination? Maybe instead of going to the gym, you find yourself driving towards your office. Or you are daydreaming, so you don't realize you passed your exit on the interstate. To course correct, you must first become aware you are off course.

Recognizing you are not being present is such a gift. Awareness that you are not present instantly brings you to mindfulness. Instead of shaming yourself when you notice your monkey mind or habit energy, gently acknowledge them. Try saying something like, "I see you, monkey mind." Don't try to bully or shame your monkey mind or habit energy when you notice it. Just acknowledge it. A helpful saying I came up with is "Shed your shame, and then reframe." When you start beating yourself up and shaming yourself, notice that you are shaming yourself. Let it go gently, and then reframe to be mindful. It's important to have that mentality when you notice yourself doing any of the following:

- Monkey mind
- Habit energy
- Blindly reacting
- Being judgmental toward others
- Being judgmental toward yourself
- Operating out of ego/ownership

As I said earlier, the goal of mindfulness is to be present in the moment and aware of your thoughts and feelings without being overly reactive to them. Being reactive to being reactive causes you to spiral and moves you in the opposite direction.

The first step to being less judgmental is to be aware of when you are being judgmental. You will not be able to magically stop judging yourself or others simply because you decided to. It will begin with redirecting your thoughts and attention when you notice you are being judgmental.

Get Your Head in the Game

An easy example of where mindfulness is apparent is in the world of athletics. You may have heard when they refer to top athletes as being "in the zone." Whether it's watching the ball leave the pitcher's hand heading towards the bat or studying the eyes of the opponent in the ring to try to anticipate when they are going to throw a punch, being fully present is often the difference between winning and losing.

Regardless of the sport, every seasoned athlete will tell you the same thing: take it one play at a time. What do you do in this moment? What is your intention for the next play? In this way, playing a sport is no different than playing the game of life. We want to win, but if we are focused on the end of the game, we cannot perform right now because our mind is not here right now.

"The zone" can also be thought of as a "flow" state, where you are so in the moment that time seems to stop. Artists will tell you this is how they feel when they are creating. Others describe it when they are hiking in nature. Whenever we are engaged in something we are passionate about, we tend to be fully present in that moment. Those little moments are all that matter. That's all that life is!

Similarly, when the focus shifts from the passion of the project to "winning," we lose the ability to remain present and are, once again, chasing goals to feel emotions, at least until we break the cycle.

For the Love of the Game

Randy was a man who took a lot of pride in getting his hands dirty out in the field, digging trenches, and solving problems for the customers of the regional cable company he worked for. When he got promoted into a management position and became a coaching client of mine, he shared he was struggling to learn everything and felt like he was drinking out of a firehose. He didn't feel the skills he had learned in the field were applicable in the office.

After working with him for a few sessions, it was evident that Randy was very bright and eager to do well in his new job. But as this was his first management position, he was so determined to please his new boss that if he made any errors at all, he would shame himself, often calling himself "stupid" or "an idiot." He wanted to be perfect, doing a job that he had never done before.

I tried to help him shift his perspective. "What do you do in your spare time that brings you joy?" I asked him.

"Woodworking," he said with a big smile. He shared he would spend hours building tables, chairs, and decorative pieces in the garage every weekend. He called it his second office. Sometimes, a whole Saturday would go by, and he didn't even notice.

"What happens when you sand a leg down too much?" I followed up.

"I just make another one," he answered very matter-of-factly.

"Why?"

"Well," he went on, "no sense in being bothered by it, it's all a part of the process,"

 I asked him what he meant by that.

"It happens from time to time," he said. "You try to match it up with the other legs, and you have a few backup pieces of wood ready to go in case you overshoot it." He went on to say that sometimes, he would make something decorative out of the leg that he could no longer use.

"Why don't you get angry with yourself when you have to do that?"

He didn't even hesitate, "I love the whole experience of it, and that's just part of it. If I mess up something, I ask myself what I can learn from it and go from there."

"What's so different about that and your job?"

"Other people are depending on me at my job."

"What do you feel they are depending on you for?"

Now, he paused for a moment to reflect on the question. "For me to manage my team effectively and come in under budget." "Okay, great!" I said enthusiastically. "What would it feel like if you approached your new role at work the way that you approached woodworking?"

A longer pause now. I could see the gears turning in his head as he really settled into the question.

"I would probably cut myself some damn slack," he said with a quick chuckle.

I invited him to try to be kind to himself for a week and to view work like he was working in his garage. We would then talk about how it felt during his next session.

When I let him into the Zoom meeting the following Friday, he was smiling ear to ear and holding up a picture he printed out. It was a picture of Johnny Lawrence, the karate champion villain from the first Karate Kid movie. Under the picture, he had written in Sharpie, "Sweep the leg, Johnny!"

"All right," I said with a bewildered smile. "What have we here?"

"I was doing what we talked about, and whenever I messed up, I reminded myself it was just like another leg I would work on in the garage." The enthusiasm building in his voice was undeniable. "In my mind, I told myself, ok, I'll just throw away this leg, and after a few times, in my head, it turned into 'sweep the leg.' I made this picture to hang up at my desk to make myself smile whenever I messed up."

After a few more weeks, he had shifted his mindset even more. He wasn't 'making mistakes." *He was learning.* He began to enjoy the process of working and viewed it as a skill he wanted to improve.

Ironically, by showing himself grace and enjoying the process of learning how to do his job, he became much better at it! He created a flow state by slowing down and focusing on one thing at a time with a learning mindset and being present in the moment.

About two months after he debuted his picture of Johnny, he joined one of our sessions, holding a different printout. No picture this time, just the words "THERE IS ALWAYS CAKE ON THE FLOOR" printed in a large font in all caps.

As great as the leg analogy was for showing himself grace, he expanded it to my central slogan to remind himself that there will always be situations that do not go as planned. He began utilizing this mindset in his personal life with his wife and four children. To this day, it was one of the most transformative experiences I've had with a client.

When we view the things we do with a sense of joy instead of obligation or necessity, we tend to stay in the present moment. We view the entirety of our life as a learning process. We feel an intrinsic value to our actions. By having the same love for the game of life as we do for more trivial things, we create a sense of presence and peace.

The Miracles Are in the Mundane

Life is not just the big moments—it's all the little moments in between. It's having that morning coffee with your spouse. It's chatting with the grocery store clerk who is ringing you up. We are in such a hurry to get to the big items we want to cross off our list that we forget to be present in the millions of little moments we are destined to have.

Now that I have spent several years working on my mindfulness, I am able to enjoy moments that would have caused me to lose my cool in the past. My swim around Key West was a great example. Whenever I caught my monkey mind racing (no pun intended), I calmed it down and came back to the present moment.

There were a few times when I would have thoughts like, "I still have 8 miles to swim in the ocean? How am I ever going to get there!" Whenever I was able to gain awareness of these thoughts, I gently reminded myself that all I could do was take the next stroke right at that moment. It was shifting my mindset from I "have" to keep swimming to I "get" to swim right now! I would deal with the next eight miles one stroke at a time. It didn't matter if there were eight miles or eight meters left. It would always be one stroke at a time. I would slow down and feel my fingers cutting through the water, feel the resistance of the ocean with every pull, and listen to the bubbles from my breath as I exhaled. That was the miracle in the moment.

There will come a day when I probably won't be able to swim, so why not cherish and enjoy the miracle that I am healthy enough to be able to enjoy the moment?

This same principle applies to situations we may not want to experience. When I sat there next to my best friend as the life left his body, it was one of the most painful moments of my life. But it was one that would profoundly change me and show me a deep understanding of acceptance and presence.

Part of the human experience is learning to let go of the things and the people you love. How selfish of me to not want to experience my friend's death. What was the alternative? To have him die alone? I was honored to be able to be in the moment with my friend as he left this earth.

The Glass is Already Broken

To wish we never experience any loss in our lives is to defy the human experience. Being present allows you to decide how you want to experience those moments and appreciate the people, places, and pets in your life while they are still there.

There is a story in Eastern philosophy called "The Glass is Already Broken." One day, some students came and asked their guru, "How can you be happy in a world full of impermanence?"

The guru thought for a moment, then held up his glass and said, "Someone gave me this glass. I really like this glass. It holds my water admirably, it glistens in the sun, and it rings when I touch it. One day, the wind may blow this glass off the shelf, or my elbow might knock it from the table, and it will break. When that happens, I will smile because I understand that the glass is already broken. Every moment I got to spend with it was precious. This is the way of life."

The old saying goes, ' We are born with one foot in the grave.' Everything, including you and I, is impermanent. Being mindful of each other honors that impermanence by showing care and compassion in the moments you get to experience together. If you want to live in a way where you have no regrets, whether it's a death, a breakup, or any type of separation in your life, being mindful allows you to treat everyone and everything respectfully and be present with them. If you knew this was the last time you would be with them, how would you act any differently? Would they know you loved them?

<u>Holding the Pen to Your Own Story</u>

Whether we want to think of our lives as a Choose Your Own Adventure Book or a movie, we all create a narrative of our own story. Ironically, if we are acting out of habit energy or driven by strong emotional reactions from the past, we unknowingly hand over the pen writing the story to our past. Being mindful allows us to take stock of our desire to keep living out that story. Mindfulness helps you realize that in this moment, you can choose to do something you have never done before. That doesn't mean it will be easy. But you now have a choice.

If your story has been one of victimhood, when the cake falls on the floor, it's easy to say defeatedly, "Of course, it fell! That's the story of my life." But if you are mindful, you can catch the emotional reaction and habit energy of complaining before they take hold. In that moment, the one where you have created that mindful space, you hold the pen to your own story.

Another way to consider rewriting your story is to view today as the first page. Everything in the past is prologue to this moment. After all, you can't change the facts of the past anyway. Use it to frame your present. Be fully present and decide what is the story that you want to write.

Mindfulness at Work

"I want to stop being so tied to my to-do lists," shared Brenda, one of my executive coaching clients. No matter how many things she crossed off, Brenda would often find her to-do list getting longer each day. By the time Friday rolled around, she would stay late in whichever office she had ended up in across her territory. Her routine was similar at home, immersing herself in renovations and committing to board meetings for two different local charities. She considered herself a doer.

One day, during one of our sessions, she mentioned how relaxing it was for her to sit down over the weekend and watch one of her favorite movies. I asked her what she enjoyed about it, and she shared how much the story resonated with her and brought her joy even though she had seen it many times before.

I asked her how it would feel if she started the movie, and instead of watching it, she just fast-forwarded to the credits at the end. She gave me a perplexed look, followed by, "Because then I couldn't enjoy the movie itself." The light of awareness started to go off in her head. She realized that when she is so focused on checking something off, she doesn't enjoy the process of whatever she is doing.

When she joined our video session the next week, she was all smiles. She had begun focusing on being in the moment with the things on her list, and she found she began enjoying her day so much more. And as an ironic side effect, she was able to get more done! She was focused on a single thing at a time and, in doing so, was much more effective. Yes, it was a little uncomfortable at first, and it took practice, but she eventually found the balance between setting her to-do list and finding joy in working toward its completion. She learned that it is impossible to be mindful and multitask at the same time.

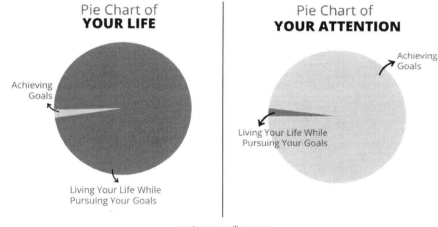

www.bergeronwellbeing.com

The Myth of Multitasking

As much as mindfulness is a superpower, multitasking is its kryptonite. In a world dominated by productivity, we often try to do several things at once, thinking we are more effective and productive. Multitasking actually moves the needle in the wrong direction. Being busier does not mean you are being more mindful or productive.

We've already explored being mindful when the cake hits the

floor. How different would it be if we started multitasking at that moment? If, instead of being in that moment and choosing to laugh or have a food fight with your husband, you grabbed a broom and started trying to sweep up the cake while talking to the caterer, demanding a refund, while your husband is trying to talk to you and your guests are trying to take pictures with you? You are doing several things instead of one and not doing any of them very well. Research has also uncovered some interesting effects of Multitasking:

- A March 2021 article in the National Library of Medicine says, "Research shows that multitasking lowers IQ, shrinks the gray matter, and lowers productivity by 40%. Conversely, mindfulness increases gray matter and improves regions involved with learning and memory processes, modulation of emotional control, and the process of awareness."
- The American Psychological Association confirmed this in an article stating, "In experiments published in 2001, Joshua Rubinstein, Ph.D., Jeffrey Evans, Ph.D., and David Meyer, Ph.D., conducted four experiments in which young adults switched between different tasks, such as solving math problems or classifying geometric objects. For all tasks, the participants lost time when they had to switch from one task to another. As tasks got more complex, participants lost more time. As a result, people took significantly longer to switch between more complex tasks."

- A third study conducted at the University of Tokyo in 2014 posits that multitasking reduces brain density in the anterior cingulate cortex at the back of the brain. That's the region responsible for empathy and emotional control.

Don't Confuse Distractions for Actions

Bragging because you are doing 27 things at once prevents you from enjoying any one of those at the moment. Sometimes, without even realizing it, we engage in so many activities because it distracts us from feeling those emotions that we label as "bad." That is the exact opposite of mindfulness. In order to release the feeling, it is important to feel it. Keeping yourself so busy that you do not process things is no different than any other addiction. You are chronically engaging in an activity to prevent yourself from feeling what is arising for you at that moment.

Tools to Help You Be Mindful

Think of mindfulness as a goal for the mind, like staying in shape is for the body. You need to know what tools to use, how to use them, and have a consistent ritual. If you have never exercised regularly, you cannot expect to get in shape overnight. It's a process. Also, like getting in shape, it's not as effective if you wait until you urgently need the tools. If the highest you usually get your heart rate is when you walk from the couch to the fridge, deciding to start a cardio routine when you see a bear come over the hill during your hike won't really benefit you. Sure, the catabolic energy will help you, but keeping yourself physically strong before encountering a bear is probably ideal.

Similarly, mindful techniques are the most beneficial when you use them regularly, not just when you are already in a catabolic state. Try using one or more of these tools on a regular basis to help increase your mindfulness. Even though I have listed scenarios when certain techniques may be helpful, I recommend you make time to use them regularly so they can be more beneficial in times of crisis.

Tool: Engage Your Senses (5-4-3-2-1)

When to use it: When you find yourself in a panicked state or your mind is drifting off.

By engaging all of your senses in the present moment, you can bring your mind back to now. This is a technique commonly used to help those with PTSD to calm their mind, especially when we get lost in fear or our own imagination. The technique is as follows:

IN THIS MOMENT, what are:

- *5 things you can see*
- *4 things you can touch*
- *3 things you can hear*
- *2 things you can smell*
- *1 thing you can taste*

Try it right now. Stop reading this book for a moment and use this method to engage all of your senses.

Here is what I am engaging with in this moment of writing this book:

- 5 things I see: A monitor, a dog, a tree, a fountain, and a glass of water
- 4 things I can touch (and that I DO reach out and touch): the glass of water, my dog, a lamp, my desk.
- 3 things I can hear: a fan, my dog snoring, and the clack of the keyboard keys as I type.
- 2 things I can smell: my deodorant and the rain outside.
- 1 thing I can taste: My coffee from this morning.

Now, I'm here in this moment. Stop reading for a moment and try this now, wherever you are. You can incorporate this with other activities like going for a walk, eating, or exercising to bring your mind and body together to the present moment. This creates space and gives you complete freedom to determine how you want to respond.

Breathing Techniques

Your breath is with you from the moment you are born till the moment you die. It's also one of the only things you can control consciously or subconsciously. Both of these facts make it the perfect focus to help you return to this moment. Here are a few that you may find helpful depending on the situation or the goal. Don't worry about mastering them all (or even "mastering" one of them). Choose one and practice it for a few minutes daily, even if you don't feel stressed.

Tool: Mindful Breathing

When to use it: *When you find yourself in stressful situations.*

Mindful breathing is one of the simplest yet most effective techniques for pausing before reacting. This technique is excellent when you find yourself in the middle of a stressful situation. When emotions are running high and automatic reactions seem inevitable, taking a few deliberate breaths can be a game-changer.

Here's how it works:

1. *Find a quiet and comfortable space if possible, (but this can be practiced anywhere).*
2. *Close your eyes if you feel comfortable doing so.*
3. *Take a slow, deep breath through your nose, counting to four as you inhale. Feel the breath filling your lungs.*
4. *Hold your breath for a count of two.*
5. *Exhale slowly and completely through your mouth, counting to six as you release the breath.*

Repeat this process a few times. As you focus on your breath, you create a pause in the flurry of thoughts and emotions. This pause allows you to regain composure, center yourself, and choose your response consciously.

Tool: Deep Diaphragmatic Breathing

When to use it:

- *Use this technique when you need to reduce stress or anxiety quickly.*
- *Before a challenging conversation or presentation, stay calm and focused.*
- *Incorporate it into your daily routine as a grounding exercise.*

Steps:

1. *Find a quiet and comfortable space to sit or lie down.*
2. *Place one hand on your chest and the other on your abdomen.*
3. *Inhale deeply through your nose, allowing your abdomen to rise while keeping your chest relatively still.*
4. *Exhale slowly through your mouth or nose, feeling your abdomen fall.*
5. *Continue this deep diaphragmatic breathing for several minutes.*

Tool: Box Breathing (Four-Square Breathing)

When to Use It:

- *When you need to regain composure during moments of stress or intense emotions.*
- *To enhance focus and concentration, making it suitable for tasks requiring mental clarity.*
- *Before bedtime to calm the mind and promote better sleep.*

Steps:

1. *Sit comfortably with your back straight.*
2. *Inhale through your nose for a count of four.*
3. *Hold your breath for a count of four.*
4. *Exhale through your nose for a count of four.*
5. *Pause and hold your breath for a count of four.*
6. *Repeat this cycle several times.*

Tool: 4-7-8 Breathing (Relaxing Breath)

When to use it:

- *For relaxation and stress reduction, making it ideal for managing anxiety or before a challenging situation.*
- *To ease into a state of deep relaxation before bedtime.*

Steps:

1. *Begin by sitting or lying down in a comfortable position.*
2. *Close your eyes and take a deep breath in through your nose for a count of four.*
3. *Hold your breath for a count of seven.*

4. *Exhale slowly through your mouth for a count of eight, making a gentle whooshing sound.*
5. *Repeat this cycle three more times.*

Experiment with each one to discover which one resonates with you the most, and practice regularly to experience the transformative power of mindful breathing in various situations. Whether you need to reduce stress, enhance concentration, or find inner peace, the art of mindful breathing will serve you on your journey to mindfulness and self-improvement, helping you in every moment, even when there's cake on the floor.

CHAPTER 7 REFLECTION QUESTIONS

Mindfulness and Present Moment Awareness:

Reflecting on your own life, how often do you find yourself caught up in thoughts about the past or worries about the future rather than fully experiencing the present moment?

Coping with Unexpected Events:

Consider a recent event in your life where something didn't go as planned. How did you react in that moment? Were you able to maintain a sense of presence and acceptance, or did you find yourself getting caught up in frustration or disappointment?

Finding Joy and Purpose:

Think about a task or responsibility in your life that you approach with a sense of obligation or necessity rather than joy. How might your experience of that task change if you were to approach it with the same enthusiasm and curiosity as you would a hobby or passion?

Self-Compassion and Learning Mindset:

Have there been instances in your life where you've been overly critical of yourself for making mistakes or not meeting expectations? How might adopting a mindset of self-compassion and learning, as described in the chapter, influence your approach to challenges or setbacks?

Embracing Impermanence and Cherishing Moments:
Consider the concept of "The Glass is Already Broken." How does this idea resonate with you, especially in terms of embracing impermanence and cherishing moments with loved ones?

Rewriting Your Life Narrative:
Reflect on the narrative of your own life story. Are there aspects of your past experiences or habits that have been shaping your present reality without your conscious awareness? How might cultivating mindfulness empower you to rewrite aspects of your story and make more intentional choices in the present?

CHAPTER 8

MEDITATION

THE GOAL OF MEDITATION ISN'T TO CONTROL YOUR
THOUGHTS, IT'S TO STOP LETTING THEM CONTROL YOU.

— S.N. GOENKA

If mindfulness is fitness for the mind, then meditation is a state-of-the-art health club. While most of the mindfulness tools I list in the last chapter can be done anywhere at any time, meditation is (usually) more ritualistic.

With the constant turmoil that is going on inside your mind, you can see why it is so hard to attain mindfulness. Emotions, thoughts, and sensations are all raging around like the rapids of a fast-moving river. If you are standing at the edge of the water looking in, the turbulence makes it impossible to see the bottom. If you walk down the banks to where the water is calmer, it becomes clear. Your mind is the same way. In order to see things clearly, you have to learn to calm the mind down. Meditation is the best way to do that.

Be Gentle

The way to calm the mind may sound counterintuitive. You cannot force your mind into submission. It's as effective as telling an angry person to "calm down." When you give an angry person space to vent, they tend to calm down much faster than when they are ordered to calm down.

You can also think of your mind as a jar of muddy water. The more you pick up and shake it around, trying to see what's in it, the more you agitate it. The way to clear the water is to let the jar sit there, and eventually, all the mud will sink to the bottom, leaving the water clear.

Instead of forcing the mind to bend to your will, when you gain awareness of the chaos and observe it without judgment, it settles on its own. When I attended the 10-day Vipassana meditation course, the first three days consisted of concentrating on the breath coming out of the nostrils to help calm the mind. As life-changing and helpful as I found ten days of meditation, I'm not advocating for that as your starting point. There are simple meditation practices you can do daily in your own home or at work. But remember, simple doesn't mean easy. So, before I get into the specifics of what meditation is, it may be easier to start with what meditation is not.

What Meditation is Not

- **Meditation is not achievable in 5-minute Increments.**

  Trying to meditate for 5 minutes is like trying to boil water a minute a day. Allowing the mind to settle takes time. A Zen proverb says you should meditate for 20 minutes a day, and if you don't have the time for that, you should meditate for an hour. Part of the point of meditation is to allow you to be more present, and if you cram your day so full of activities that you don't have 20 minutes to dedicate to your mental well-being, odds are, you are doing too much (and none of it well).

- **Meditation is not having an empty mind**

  When I first began meditation, I made the common mistake of thinking that the point was to think about nothing. Though it may be possible to have an empty mind in higher states of meditation, the most common forms of meditation involve awareness of the thoughts instead of removing them. We've already established that thoughts think themselves. Meditation is the awareness of the thought. The gentle acknowledgment that "ok, there is a thought." Then, releasing it without judgment and returning to the breath.

- **Meditation is not relaxation**

  If your idea of meditating is closing your eyes for a few minutes and breathing before falling asleep, that is not meditation. It could be considered mindfulness, depending on your focus. Though meditation can be relaxing, relaxing, in and of itself, is not meditation.

What meditation IS:

- **Meditation is focusing your awareness on a single thing**

  Whether it is the breath, a focal point, a mantra, a visual image, or a sensation in the body, meditation is focused attention. The aim is to cultivate a deep and undistracted level of awareness, allowing the meditator to become fully present in the chosen moment. At the same time, all other thoughts and distractions fade into the background just as the mud settles to the bottom of the jar.

- **Meditation is observing your thoughts and feelings without judgment**

  At its core, meditation involves the practice of observing thoughts and feelings without judgment. Rather than getting entangled or carried away by the content of your mental activity, the purpose is to step back and become impartial observers. In this state, thoughts and emotions are acknowledged as they arise, but without attaching labels like "good" or "bad," "right" or "wrong." A thought is just a thought. That's why understanding the difference between fact and judgment is so critical. It allows you to look at a thought objectively without bias, giving you a sense of neutrality and peace. If you are focused on your breath and you notice you are thinking, that's okay. Acknowledge the thought and return your attention to the breath gently, without judgment of yourself or the thought. Just as the only way to know you are lost is to have the realization you are off course, the only way to strengthen your mindfulness is to have an awareness of when you have shifted your attention to thought. That's a gift! You now have the ability to gently direct your awareness away from the thought and back to the breath.

- **Meditation is developing awareness**
  Meditation is fundamentally about developing awareness of oneself and the world around you. By gaining awareness of the true nature of your thoughts and emotions, you realize you are separate from them and do not have to follow their bidding blindly. This is what gives you the space… the wonderful, magical pause that allows you to respond to the cake on the floor.

Types of Meditation

This is, by no means, an exhaustive list of all the different types of meditation. There are many different types that have different focuses. Some help you visualize peace by sending out meta-loving-kindness. Others focus on visualization techniques to elicit positive feelings. Most of the types I recommend here are designed to help you notice without judging any thoughts or feelings that arise. Though the other types of meditation will also help you practice non-judgment, these are the ones that have the greatest impact on your ability to pause. These are just a few of the types of meditation I recommend.

Tool: Mindfulness Meditation

What to Use It For: *Mindfulness meditation is helpful for developing present-moment awareness, reducing stress, and enhancing overall well-being.*

Steps:
- *Find a quiet and comfortable space.*
- *Close your eyes if you feel comfortable doing so.*
- *Focus your attention on your breath or a specific point of awareness (e.g., sensations in your body, sounds, or a mantra).*
- *When your mind wanders (as it inevitably will), gently bring your focus back to your chosen point of awareness without judgment.*
- *Continue this process for a designated period, gradually increasing the duration as you become more comfortable.*

Tool: Vipassana Meditation

What to Use It For: *Vipassana meditation is helpful for gaining insight into the nature of reality, self-awareness, and personal transformation.*

Steps:
- *Find a quiet and comfortable place to sit.*

- *Close your eyes and focus on your breath, observing the natural rhythm of inhalation and exhalation.*
- *Shift your awareness to bodily sensations, starting with your head and moving down to your toes, observing any tension, discomfort, or sensations without reacting.*
- *As thoughts or emotions arise, acknowledge them and return your focus to bodily sensations.*
- *Continue this process, gradually expanding your awareness to include external sounds and sensations while maintaining a non-reactive stance.*

Tool: Gratitude Meditation

What to Use It For: *Gratitude meditation is helpful for cultivating a positive mindset, reducing negativity, and enhancing overall well-being.*

Steps:

- *Find a quiet and comfortable place to sit or lie down.*
- *Close your eyes and take a few deep breaths to relax.*
- *Bring your attention to the present moment and reflect on what you're grateful for.*
- *Start with small things, like the warmth of the sun or a pleasant interaction you had today, and gradually move to bigger things.*

- *As you focus on each source of gratitude, explore the feelings of appreciation and positivity associated with them.*
- *Continue this practice for a designated period, ending with a deep breath and a sense of contentment.*

These meditation techniques offer different approaches to self-improvement and can be powerful tools. If I were to recommend one of them to start, it would be mindfulness meditation.

Easy Does It

When you begin your meditation practice, a common trap is to get angry with yourself whenever you notice thoughts coming into your head. When this happens, remember, we have established throughout this book that thoughts think themselves. The key to mindfulness meditation is to notice the thought, release it without judgment, and return to the breath. I used the analogy earlier in the book and will use it again here. It's like lifting weights to get stronger. You will not be able to release every thought without judgment when you first begin meditation, much like you won't be able to bench press 200 lbs. your first time. Start wherever you are at.

The goal isn't perfection. The goal is progress. The more you are able to notice thoughts without judgment and release them during meditation, the more you can detach from thoughts during stressful situations and increase the pause, allowing you to respond instead of react.

The Best of Times, the Worst of Times

I wasn't quite prepared for what a roller coaster of experiences the 10-day meditation course would be. The first few days, though challenging, were a welcomed break from the hustle of life at home. I would wake up at four am and go for a short 15-minute walk on the desert trail behind my dorm. The predawn sky was incredible, and seeing the millions of stars over the desert mountains helped me get my mindset right before joining the other students in the meditation hall by 4:30 am.

By the fourth day, my monkey mind had enough. It was bored, cranky, and tired of me sitting and observing it. The more I tried to force it to be quiet, the louder it got. Around the end of day five, I decided to let it scream all it wanted. I just noticed it. I didn't judge it or tell it to be quiet; I just observed it and returned to scanning my body in the style of Vipassana.
At the end of day seven, something happened as I lay in my cell for my final hour of meditation before bed: I had, in all sincerity, a moment of enlightenment—true transcendence, where I felt connected to everyone and everything.

Finally, everything in the universe made sense by just sitting and observing my thoughts, feelings, and sensations in my body. And just as quickly as that moment arrived, it was gone.

I returned to the meditation hall the following day, crying tears of joy. I couldn't wait to feel that experience again. I sat down, closed my eyes, and began my 'sits of determination.'* I felt the energy course through me like Dr Strange. As powerful a feeling as it was, it was nowhere near the experience I had the night before. So, I tried even harder. I did everything I could to return to that blissful oneness. The harder I tried, the more my monkey mind raged.

What I didn't realize at the time was that I was chasing a feeling instead of simply observing what I was feeling at the moment, ironically driving me further away from being present. By trying to make my mind have a different experience, I was denying it the experience it was having. I was missing the whole point.

Thich Nhat Hahn famously said, *"On the way to enlightenment, chop wood and carry water. Once you have reached enlightenment, chop wood and carry water."* Enlightenment is an understanding, not a permanent state of awareness. But I

"Sits of Determination" is to remain completely still while meditating, regardless of what is going on with your body. If you feel an itch, you notice the itch without judgment. No itch has lasted forever. By simply observing it, it allows you to strengthen your non-judgment.

wanted sooo badly to feel it again.

It's often said that the worst meditation session you will ever have is right after you're most enlightened. Because now you are chasing that experience and not just observing the reality of your present mind in that moment. Allow each session to be Whatever it is for that session. Sometimes, it will feel incredible, and sometimes, it will feel exhausting. Allow it to be whatever it is.

There's a Zen saying about a man who goes to seek a guru and asks, "Master, how long will I have to study with you to be a Zen Master of my own?"

"Five years," replied the guru.

"What if I try really hard? If I put all of my effort into becoming enlightened and walking the path?"

"Ah. In that case? Ten years."

Meditation is the act of observing and letting go, not forcing. Allow each experience to be whatever it is. Be kind to yourself in this journey. Remember, instead of self-improvement, focus on self-compassion.

CHAPTER 8 REFLECTION QUESTIONS

Understanding Meditation:

How do you perceive the relationship between mindfulness and meditation based on the chapter's analogy of fitness and a health club?

In what ways does the analogy of a jar of muddy water resonate with your understanding of calming the mind through meditation?

Common Misconceptions:

Reflect on your previous assumptions about meditation. How do they align or diverge from the explanations provided in the chapter?

Have you ever attempted meditation in short increments, such as 5 minutes? What was your experience, and how does it compare to the chapter's perspective?

Core Principles of Meditation

How do you interpret the concept of "focusing your awareness on a single thing" in meditation? How might this practice foster mindfulness?

Consider your experiences with thoughts and emotions during meditation. How do you currently approach them, and how might the chapter's insights influence your practice?

Types of Meditation:

Reflect on the three types of meditation introduced in the chapter (Mindfulness, Vipassana, and Gratitude). Which one resonates with you the most, and why?

How might you incorporate gratitude meditation into your daily routine based on the steps provided in the chapter?

Starting Your Meditation Journey

Evaluate your attitude towards beginner's challenges in meditation, such as managing intrusive thoughts. How might the chapter's encouragement to embrace imperfection impact your approach?

Reflect on the distinction between self-improvement and self-compassion in the context of meditation. How can you integrate this perspective into your practice?

CHAPTER 9

ADDITIONAL TOOLS

"WE SHAPE OUR TOOLS, AND THEREAFTER OUR TOOLS SHAPE US."

— MARSHALL MCLUHAN

Recently, a friend shared an idea over lunch that I found pretty innovative. A mother of two young girls, she was committed to teaching her girls how to navigate the world's challenges in a mindful way. "I made them a toolbelt," she said. I asked her what she meant.

She told me how she had gone out and gotten a children's set of play carpenter tools. Whenever she taught her girls a new life skill, they would take a marker and write the name of that skill on a specific tool. That way, whenever the girls had a problem, they would think about what tools they had at their disposal to use the one that might best be suited for the job.

In this chapter, I want to provide more tools to help you in any cake-on-the-floor situation. Some of these are of my own creation, and some are not, but each one is helpful depending on the job you need it for. These tools require a little more explanation than the other tools in the book, so they are formatted differently to provide clarity.

Tool #1: The C.A.L.M. Method

This is a tool I created to help people, well, calm down in stressful situations. It combines four different elements to help you move from reacting to responding. C.A.L.M. stands for Center, Awareness, Learn, and Mantra.

Center - The first thing to do when encountering a stressful situation is to center yourself. This can be done with any of the techniques in the mindfulness chapter. It's not a full meditation, but it takes anywhere from a few seconds to up to five minutes of mindful breathing, counting, walking, or anything to create that magical pause between you and the thing that just upset you.

Awareness- Once you are centered, you can gain awareness of the facts and the judgments of the situation. Separate them out! Remember, strong emotions come from judging the facts, not the facts themselves. Gain awareness of the story that you are telling yourself. How accurate is it?

Learn- What can you learn from this situation? Focus on whatever the lesson is rather than the loss. Ask yourself if your feelings are based on this moment or rooted in a past event. How do you want your response to this moment to define you?

Mantra- What helpful phrase can you use to ground yourself and find peace in this situation? To create an effective mantra:
- Turn negatives into positives
- Use present tense
- Say it with feeling

For example, if your cake falls to the floor and you feel angry, say, "I am calm," or "This too shall pass." Other examples of mantras are:
- I am peace
- I am loved
- I am happy
- I can conquer my fears

Tool #2: Just F It

Another tool I developed, this one helps me and my clients who are stuck in victim mode or don't know how to move past a situation. Where the C.A.L.M. method works better for an immediate stressor, I use Just F It when dealing with a longer-term block or issue. This tool can also be implemented as a journal entry.

Just F It consists of four F's: Feelings, Facts, Flip it, and Future.

The first F is for feelings.

I like to do this immediately after I have centered or sometimes while centering.

As discussed in the chapter on emotions, the more we can understand and articulate how we feel accurately, the better we learn from our feelings.

Once you are able to identify what you are feeling, ask yourself *where* you are feeling it. If you are feeling frustrated, where in your body do you notice the change? Is it tension behind your eyes, a tightening in your chest?

Developing awareness about where the feeling "lives" in your body will help you identify it faster in the future and develop techniques to relax or dissipate the energy more quickly.

The second F is for facts.

Again, objectively separate the facts from the judgments. You get the idea by now.

The third F is for flip it.

While the first two F's help you understand what you are feeling and the reality of the current situation, the next two F's help you be more solution-focused by allowing you to experience other perspectives. The first of these two is "flip it." What I mean by that is to flip the story you are currently telling yourself about the situation and view it from the opposing perspective. Sometimes, the feelings can feel so overwhelming that we get stuck. By flipping it, we can see solutions and get unstuck.

To give you an example, a little over a year ago, I had a hard time dealing with a bad breakup. I was spiraling into a depressive state and was unsure how to snap out of it. While sitting around a bonfire reflecting on my state, a thought occurred to me as I was grieving. "*What if* I wasn't grieving? What would that look like? How would I feel? What actions would I take?"

Asking myself those simple questions allowed me to get out of my own head and think about another point of view. It helped remind me that my current feelings would not last forever. If I wasn't grieving, I could move on with my life. I could enjoy this bonfire and feel more fulfilled with friends. I would be able to spend the energy currently invested in grieving on my healing. I was capable of feeling and acting differently. Flipping it created just enough space between me and the story for me to realize I had options.

The fourth F is for future.
What advice would the 80-year-old version of yourself (or, if you are already 80, the 90-year-old version) give you in this

situation? What would the future version of yourself say that you did in this situation that helped mold you into the best possible version of yourself? Not only does this allow us to view the situation a little more objectively, but it inherently taps into the wisest version of ourselves for answers. Generally, we already have the answers within us, and this creates space to allow us to access it.

To help illustrate this point, think about what advice CURRENT you would have given your younger self in certain pivotal situations you went through. Don't view this as an exercise where you are trying to change the past, but more as one to help you realize that the older you get, the wiser you get. Your perspective tends to broaden to view more solutions and be less reactionary.

Tool #3: The Five Remembrances

This tool comes from someone much further along the path than myself. First taught by the Buddha over 2,000 years ago, the Five Remembrances are five facts about life and reality designed to help you keep things in perspective.

I keep a copy of them on my nightstand. Reading them before I get out of bed in the morning allows me to practice gratitude for what I have in my life. Reflecting on them before I go to bed helps me come back to reality in a way that allows me to be present and practice acceptance in a way that helps me fall asleep with peace in my heart.

Even though these are facts, I didn't introduce them in the chapter on Facts vs Judgment because I wanted to ensure we explored mindfulness before addressing them. They are as follows:

The Five Remembrances

- I am of the nature to grow old. There is no way to escape growing old.
- I am of the nature to have ill health. There is no way to escape having ill health.
- I am of the nature to die. There is no way to escape death.
- All that is dear to me and everyone I love are of the nature to change. There is no way to escape being separated from them.
- My actions are my only true belongings. I cannot escape the consequences of my actions. My actions are the ground upon which I stand.

At first, they may seem depressing or disappointing. You may ask yourself, "Why the hell would I want to remember that?" Because they help you find gratitude for what you do have in the present moment. As uncomfortable as they may be, learning to accept them as facts is the key to accepting the cake on the floor.

Let's look at each one individually. But to help their importance sink in, instead of calling them remembrances, I will refer to them as facts.

Fact #1: I am of the nature to grow old. There is no way to escape growing old.

When I first started DJing weddings in Arkansas, I would play Strawberry Wine by Deana Carter almost every weekend. I remember singing along as a teenager and chuckling at her lyrics, "I still remember when 30 was old." Thirty *was* old! Oh, the irony.

Twenty-five years later, I could be upset that I am no longer that youthful, energetic boy with a full head of hair ready to take on the world. But that's just a denial of what age I am now. As the great philosopher Popeye once said, "I am what I am." Well, right now, I am forty-four. Sure, there may be a day when I can no longer swim, drive, or walk. But that's not today. If I ever make it to 85, I may regret the things that I did not do at forty-four because I was so upset that I'm not a teenager anymore. By judging that I am not as young as I used to be, I deny myself the ability to appreciate the youth, energy, and ability I have at forty-four.

Fact #2: I am of the nature to have ill health. There is no way to escape having ill health.

Injury and illness are facts of life. We know this to be accurate, but we get so upset when they inevitably happen! By accepting the fact that we are ill or injured, we can focus on the things we can do. Have a bad cold and can't go to work? Instead of being upset you are sick, maybe you can read a book you've meant to.

Even if it's hard to find a silver lining when we are sick, this fact helps us learn to appreciate our health when we are not ill or injured. When I reflect on how much pain I was in with herniated discs in my back and being unable to walk, I have gratitude for my current physical condition.

Fact #3: I am of the nature to die. There is no way to escape death

So many of us are so uncomfortable at the thought we will die one day that we do everything we can to avoid thinking about it. We view death like an ostrich with its head buried in the sand. We don't want to talk about it or think about it. We get sad or uncomfortable when someone else mentions it. But the fact is we are all going to die.

On my office wall, I have a large poster that has 52 rows across and 85 lines down. At the top of the poster, in large lettering, are the Latin words "Memento Mori," a concept lived by the Roman Stoic Marcus Aurelius, which literally translates to "remember that you will die." Every week, I fill in another circle, indicating another of the 52 weeks of that year of my life has passed.

I don't know when it will be the last time I fill in a circle. But I do know that I am alive today.* The fact that I will die one day can either paralyze me with fear or allow me to be grateful and appreciate that I am alive today.

Now. At this moment. I am the glass that is already broken. What's the point in pretending I am never going to die? How is that helpful? So, while here, I want to be present and learn to love this moment.

These first three remembrances are designed to strip us of our childlike naivety that we will live forever. We waste our time and energy and become upset when we inevitably grow older, get sick, or face death.

Fact 4: All that is dear to me and everyone I love are of the nature to change. There is no way to escape being separated from them.

This fact alone hits us right in the ego. We want to hold onto the things and people that we love forever. We want them to always be with us. This, again, ties back into the glass is already broken. Realizing that everyone and everything is impermanent allows us to treat them with heartfelt respect and compassion in this moment.

At least as of the writing of this book. Should you be reading this after I am gone, then this book is a Memento of my Mori. I leave it to you as a token of my legacy.

Fact #5: My actions are my only true belongings. I cannot escape the consequences of my actions. My actions are the ground upon which I stand.

Think back to the section on ownership in Chapter 6. At the end of the day, the only thing you really own is the consequences of your actions. *All the more reason to learn how to respond instead of reacting to the cake on the floor!!* This is essentially the lesson of the book. How you respond or react to the cake on the floor is what will determine who you are. Sorry, it took nine chapters to have it stated so succinctly.

CHAPTER 9 REFLECTION QUESTIONS

On Using Tools in Life's Challenges:
Reflect on a challenging situation you've encountered recently. How did you initially approach it? Did you consider the tools at your disposal, metaphorically speaking, like the toolbelt described by the mother in the chapter?

The C.A.L.M. Method:
Try the C.A.L.M. Method next time you are in a stressful situation. How effective was it in helping you move from reacting to responding? If not, how might you apply it in future challenges?

Just F It:
Think of a situation where you felt stuck in victim mode or couldn't move past an issue. How might applying the Just F It method help you gain perspective and find solutions?

The Five Remembrances:
Consider each of the Five Remembrances individually. Which one resonates with you the most, and why? How might embracing these truths about life enhance your perspective and approach to challenges?

Taking Action:
Reflect on a recent situation where you were challenged

to respond instead of react. How did you handle it, and what were the outcomes? How might applying the lessons from this chapter influence your future actions in similar circumstances?

CHAPTER 10

CONCLUSION

"IF YOU WANT A HAPPY ENDING, THAT DEPENDS, OF COURSE,
ON WHERE YOU STOP THE STORY."

— ORSON WELLES

"Of course you did, you're Ramsey."

I've heard that numerous times throughout my adult life. When
someone heard about one of my accomplishments, they
chalked it up to some divine blessing, allowing me to coast
through life and preventing me from encountering any
hardships. As I've shared throughout this book, that has not at
all been the case.

What has allowed me to rise above the challenges I endured was my perspective. My ability to make the most of situations that were outside of my control. When people did learn of my hardships, they asked me how I did it. I remember telling them I didn't have a choice. That it was the only way I could survive. Only now, as I finish writing this book, do I realize that it *was* a choice.

So many people allow their hardships to define them. They craft them into their story. Or, worse yet, they allow challenges to defeat them. I wrote this book to help those of you who want to rise above the circumstance's life has thrown at you and not let them define you.

Having the tools to handle stress doesn't prevent you from encountering it. Otherwise, what good would the tools be if you never got a chance to use them? Ships are safe in the harbor, but that's not what ships are built for. Use these tools to sail away from the shores of complacency to discover what you are really made of during life's most arduous tests.

Be kind to yourself in this process. As cliche as it sounds, life is all about the journey. What are you in such a hurry for? Why are you striving to be perfect? Let the situation be what it will be. Embrace the present moment.

At the same time, don't sit back and let life happen to you. What do you intend to do with the intellectual understanding you have gained reading this book?

One of my favorite parables I share with my clients is a riddle. Ten birds are sitting on a wire, and five decide to fly away. How many are left on the wire?

The answer is ten.

Just because the birds *decided* to fly away doesn't mean they did anything.

Take action. Be intentional with your life by practicing mindfulness and compassion. And again, instead of self-improvement, focus on self-compassion. That doesn't absolve us from the consequences of our actions, but it allows us to find peace in our humanity.

In pursuing a meaningful life of growth and connection, the hardest tightrope we will ever walk is between accountability and grace. It's a balance that may take our whole lives to master. But that's okay. What else will we do with the time other than live it? To be present in the moment with it.

Being present allows you to respond to stressors in a way that aligns with your values. It's the difference between screaming that your wedding is ruined and having a food fight with three hundred of your closest friends. Because in life, there is always cake on the floor.

ABOUT THE AUTHOR

Ramsey Bergeron is a certified Leadership and Mindset Coach, skilled facilitator, and published author with over 15 years of experience in the coaching and wellness industries. His journey began in a Memphis nightclub, and within five years, he worked his way up to become a National Director of Field Marketing for over twenty clubs across the country. In 2006, Ramsey pivoted and dedicated his life to health and well-being.

Ramsey's diverse clientele includes CEOs, professional athletes, and individuals seeking self-improvement. A few of his accomplishments during his time in the fitness industry include completing eight Ironman races, leading adventure retreats worldwide, and serving as a national spokesperson for EAS Sports Nutrition.

An ICF Certified Professional Coach with numerous certifications, Ramsey is committed to personal growth, which is evident in his participation in a 10-day silent meditation course and swimming 12.5 miles around Key West. Beyond professional pursuits, he gives back through charity work and enjoys life in Scottsdale, AZ, with his two rescue dogs and red-eared slider.

Cake on the Floor

The emcee, in complete shock, doesn't have time to pull out the winning ticket before Gallager smashes the cake.

Your egoic monkey mind starts to swing from branch to branch, playing the what-if game. What if it was your cake? What if you were supposed to win it, but now you never will?

You don't know if you should be upset or not. Should you be upset? Were you going to win it? This seems more like an Andy Kaufman bit than a Gallager bit. Your brain tries to create a story around what happened, but without knowing if you won the cake or not, you are unsure how to feel about it.

You are unable to determine how you should feel about it, so the whole situation lives in your mind much longer because you don't know how to process it. You are stuck because you need to know if it was your cake to decide how you feel about it. Without that knowledge, your brain is stuck in a loop.

Years later in therapy, you manage to get out of the loop when you finally conclude that:

1. You never owned the cake.
2. You accepted the facts of what happened that day.
3. It's okay that you will never have the answers you were looking for, and you create your own closure, realizing there is always cake on the floor.

(Turn to page 109)

Cake on the Floor

The emcee draws the winning ticket belonging to a stranger, and then Gallager smashes the cake.

What a show! Since you didn't win, you felt no sense of attachment to the cake. It was not your cake. Sure, you may be a little disappointed you didn't win, but watching the cake splatter all over the crowd was entertaining. You didn't happen to notice who did win, and maybe you feel a little bad for them. You may even have a sense of relief that you didn't win. Could you imagine winning and having your cake smashed? At the end of the day, you have a story about watching a cake get splattered.

(Turn to page 109)

Cake on the Floor

The emcee draws the winning ticket belonging to Susan Spiteful, the person you dislike more than anyone else in the world, and then Gallager smashes the cake.

Best. Day. Ever.

The look on Susan's face when that sledgehammer came down on her cake made the rollercoaster of emotions worth it. Your disappointment at not winning the cake is replaced with glee, watching her cry. You take pictures of the destroyed cake and her tears and text them to your friends. You feel such joy at her loss that you forget all about wanting to win the very same cake. Once you realized she had won it, you secretly wished for its destruction. In your mind, Gallager was obviously sent by the Lord himself to carry out this karmic retribution on your nemesis. You high-five him as you exit the auditorium.

(Turn to page 109)

Cake on the Floor

The emcee draws the ticket, and you find out you won the cake before Gallager smashes it.

When the emcee announces your number, a dopamine hit causes you to feel elated! You've won! That is now your cake up on the stage!

But then, as you see Gallager wind up the sledgehammer, bringing it down full steam, sending a spray of liquified sugar to cover the closest three rows in the audience. Your ecstasy transitions to sadness. Perhaps even anger! How dare he do this to your cake! The emcee selected your ticket, and this cake belonged to you! Never mind the fact that you weren't even getting married. The fact that you've been single with three cats for over a year is beside the point. It was your cake! But now, it's gone.

Defeated, sad, and cakeless, you throw the ticket in the garbage and exit the auditorium with your head hung low.

(Turn to page 109)

Looking for additional tools and resources from Ramsey Bergeron? Scan here!

Cake on the Floor

Made in the USA
Monee, IL
29 March 2024

b8947a3b-aaa5-439a-a135-c5ca78520657R01